CW00448652

# THE JOSHUA PROJECT

**by Kingsley N. Armstrong**

BARRATT MINISTRIES PUBLICATIONS
Manchester M14 5QH, England

For further copies of this book or for more information about The Joshua Project, contact:
**www.thejoshuaproject.co.uk**
email: **kingsley@thejoshuaproject.co.uk**



**THE JOSHUA PROJECT**
by **Kingsley N. Armstrong**

**British Library Cataloguing-in-Publication Data**

A catalogue record for this book is available from the British Library

ISBN: 1 904592 09 0

Published by **Barratt Ministries Publications**
114 Daisy Bank Road, Victoria Park, Manchester M14 5QH, UK.
E-mail: info@barrattministries.org.uk
Web: www.barrattministries.org.uk

# Contents

# Acknowledgements

I want to thank ...

... God for making this book possible. He is the inspiration behind the Joshua Project and the One who holds it all together.

... Cathy for being the most incredibly patient wife in the world. I sometimes wonder how she manages to put up with me! But I guess that's what best friends are for.

... My children, Jemima and Isaac, for allowing me to do what God has called me to do, and for always being there when I get back home.

... Rodney and Jeanette and all at New Life Baptist Church in Northallerton for being such a tremendous support to us as a family.

... Bob and Ann and my friends in International Gospel Outreach for the constant encouragement, and my mum for our Sunday night chats!

... All at Barratt Ministries and especially Alex who has helped me put this book together.

I know that I am a blessed man and I appreciate it. Thank you!

# Foreword

In the many years I have known Kingsley, I have never ceased to marvel at his consistency and the simplicity of his faith in the living God. For Kingsley, *if God said it* - that is sufficient - and contrary circumstances are irrelevant! He has always been a visionary and had big dreams and doesn't see why anyone cannot accomplish great things for God if they are willing to step out in faith on God's promises and take risks. Whenever he hears from God, nothing and no one will be able able to convince him it *'can't be done'*, or that he *'can't afford it'*. He believes that with the commission comes the provision and no matter what the need, if God has called him to a task or a Mission then it is God's responsibility to meet the need and that He will never fail to do so.

As a result, whilst many others who have similar dreams and visions wait and wait for needs to be met *before* they step out, Kingsley has been there, done it, and seen God work miracles of *provision 'as he went'*.

He is a gifted Evangelist with a world-wide ministry, and nothing thrills him more than to see multitudes turning to the Lord Jesus Christ as their Saviour and Lord. Nothing seems to faze him and he is equally at home working in areas of extreme poverty in the African, Asian or South American Countries as he is ministering to members of various Parliaments and others in high places.

His drive, enthusiasm and sincerity are plain for all to see and he is a great encourager. The Joshua Project has been used of God to liberate hundreds of believers into active and productive Christian ministry of many kinds, and I know that this book is going to help and release many thousands of people into their God-given ministries in the coming days and years.

**Rev. Bob Searle**
**General Secretary**
**International Gospel Outreach (IGO)**

# Introduction

Why a book about Joshua or indeed, why a book at all? There are two answers to that: The first is that a book can be where I cannot and can multiply the effect of the message. Secondly, I believe that the book of Joshua is such a life-changing book that all those who read it will never be the same again.

My prayer for this book is that it will be both an encouragement and an irritant; that it will inspire you to walk into the land of faith and possess all that God has for you and for those you meet. God promised Joshua that He would give him wherever he set his foot. That is also our privilege as children of God.

## Norwich Youth Camp

I guess that this book has taken me about 15 years to write as it all started at a youth camp in the summer of 1989. Mount Zion Church in Norwich is a place that I have come to love and respect over the years. I was asked to speak at one of their youth camps in a school in Lowestoft in August 1989 and we encountered tremendous spiritual opposition. I was sleeping on the floor in one of the school offices and had an experience that, thankfully I have only had twice in my Christian life. I still do not know whether I was awake or asleep but I struggled the whole night and at one stage felt that I could not even breathe. I am not afraid of the dark but a fear gripped me that night, so I got up in the early hours and walked for miles along the Norfolk Broads. When I returned to my room God spoke to me and gave me a verse, Deuteronomy 3:28 *"But commission Joshua, and encourage and strengthen him, for he will lead this people across and will cause them to inherit the land ..."* God highlighted the phrase **'cause them to inherit'** and began the process of showing me that my ministry was to lead others into the blessing and ministry that God had called them to.

Allow me to finish the story of the youth camp. The opening meeting on the night before I had this encounter was dreadful. The worship did not take off and there was a heaviness about the whole thing. I had put it down to the fact that many had travelled a long way and understandably people would be tired. I spoke for a short time and simply introduced the topic for the week (which incidentally was 'spiritual warfare'!). Then I had this dark experience and the meeting the next morning was also very heavy. However, that second night in the meeting I felt something stirring inside me and felt the urge to have all the young people shout and break through this. Just as I was dwelling on that, the leader said to everyone that we needed to shout the victory and we did. What a wonderful breakthrough we enjoyed that evening. From there on in we had a fantastic youth camp with many of the young people encountering God in a new way.

## Joshua - leading others to inherit the land

God has been speaking to me about Joshua for years. I have preached from this book more than any other and now the story has become an integral part of my life. Three incidents in particular showed how much God had that this one book more than any other written over my life.

- In 1988 during market days in Lisburn, N.Ireland, I worked in an articulated lorry that had been converted into a coffee outreach centre. Over the weeks and months we had visits from many interesting people who dropped in for a drink and we saw quite a number of folk find Christ as a result. On one particular day a man from Wales came in and sat down with some of his friends for a coffee. They had visited Hillsborough Elim Church the previous weekend and were going about the country praying for Ireland. He called me over and said that he had a word from the Lord for me. This was a strange experience for me as I was not used to people talking in such a way. He opened his Bible and read from Joshua 1:6-9, said that it was for me and then left. I never saw him again to my knowledge.

- On Jan 1st 1989 I was baptised in Woodham, Newton Aycliffe, Co. Durham. It was an amazing experience for me though I am not sure of the wisdom of allowing the actual ceremony to be carried out by one's father in law;

I am sure I was held under the water longer than the others were! However, on such occasions the pastor read a word of Scripture that they felt was relevant to the person being baptised. Pastor Glyn Greenow gave me a verse from the Lord: it was Joshua 1:9.

- In October 1991, while on holiday in Majorca and visiting the Vineyard Church, one of the young men came up to me after the meeting and said that he had a word from the Lord for me and opened his Bible to Joshua 1 and read the same verses.

I was then beginning to take notice of what the Lord was saying to me. It was obvious that the book of Joshua, especially the first chapter, had something to say to my life. I spent time studying and meditating on the book and began to see methods and processes that God used to bring His people into the land of faith. I had read many stories and biographies of people who 'lived by faith' and always found them inspiring but I longed to see this be the norm today.

As I travelled around from church to church I discovered many people who were living sleepy lives that were, in my mind, far removed from the life of faith that was possible. In particular I met people who were once enthusiastic in their teenage years but had 'retired' in their 20's and 30's. Some of them had good jobs, some were married with kids and had simply settled down. Yet in them all God had already put a spark that needed rekindling, and I wanted to help them along the way.

So in 1995 'The Joshua Project' came into being. It started off as a three-week training course in our house in North Wales and then developed into a shorter course in churches run over the period of a week. I have had the privilege of running this course in many churches throughout the British Isles, in Europe and in more recent days in Africa.

This book is based on that course and takes a close look at the first six chapters of the book of Joshua. Before you start into the first chapter, pause for a moment and ask God to come near to you and speak to you. Have your Bible close to hand and follow through the verses yourself. Be blessed as you read, then go and possess your land!

**Kingsley N. Armstrong**
**Founder of 'The Joshua Project'**

# Chapter 1

# What is your Land?

> *"Get ready to cross the Jordan River into the land I am about to give to them ... your territory will extend ... you will take possession." Joshua 1:3,4,11*

What is the land described in the book of Joshua? Obviously for Joshua, it was an actual physical place. What about for us? What does the land speak of? I believe that it is speaking of our calling, our destiny, the purpose we were created for, the reason we live.

God promises us in Jeremiah 29:11 that He has plans for our lives and that He knows those plans, plans to prosper and not to harm, plans to bring a hope and a future.

Your land could be the ministry or job that God has given you to do. It is a place full of excitement and new challenges, many giants but many blessings. The land is the place of promise for you. It is a place of potential, perhaps unrealized, yet possible! Your land is a place of adventure, of vision, of desire, of dreaming ... if only! There is more that God has for all of us, if only we could or would dare to step out of the wilderness into the land and walk.

Your land is the thing that excites you. It is the thing you dream about – and then wake up and remember that you have responsibilities and a mortgage and bills, and the cold light of day hits you with the 'realisation' that this dream is impossible. Your land is the place that puts a smile on your face and a spring in your step, the place that has your name written all over it.

**In that dream you believe the best, come out on top, and enjoy the favour of God**

In your dreamland, there is nothing you cannot do. In that dream you laugh at the impossibilities and the discouragement and keep on running for you know that it is your dream. In that dream you believe the best, come out on top, enjoy the favour of God, and succeed in everything you do, influencing men and nations. In that dream you have your eyes fixed on Jesus and walk on the water as he did. You do not have the time to look back and take heed to the criticism coming from the boat. In that dream, if only till you wake up, you have become more real than at any other time. Your excitement increased, your emotions were aroused and your feelings of fulfillment were heightened.

Let me contrast that to the very common experience of many Christians today. We love Jesus and he is alive in our hearts. We seek to follow him as best we can. We go to church on Sunday, but when we read of all the miracles that went on we are tempted to believe that it was for then and not for now. Not because our theology says it, but more because we have never seen a miracle or experienced any of the things that seemed to have gone on in Bible days. In fact there is a bit of a credibility gap between our Sunday listening and our Monday doing. To be honest many of us feel that we are stuck in dead-end jobs but we say, "What odds, it's only a job and I'm only there 'cause they pay me at the end of the month!".

Let me say this to you: read it carefully. If you are in your job simply for the money it provides for you, then I believe you are either in the wrong place, or a possessor of the wrong attitude. God never planned that you or I would waste his or our time in the wrong place just for the sake of money. For goodness sake, God can take a lunch box that cost so little and transform it into eight months of an annual income with a simple prayer! He can make a little old lady's jar of oil multiply so much that it saved her family and paid off all her debts!

When I was attending Queens University, Belfast, my wife Cathy was working in a horrible environment where the staff criticized each other, talked behind each other's backs and generally were unkind and miserable. This had an amazing effect on Cathy. She became very unhealthy and hated going to work. The atmosphere was not conducive to healthy living. We made a decision together that even though we needed the money she would give up her job before having another one lined up. Her health improved immediately and although I cannot remember how long it took to get another job, we are here today, alive and well and blessed!

**Wise up! Go out there and get a life!**

We need to work to feel fulfilled and to enjoy life. But if we are in the wrong place, all the money in the world will not compensate for it. Heading off to an office each day where we know we are going to be miserable, not wanting to be there and just counting down the hours and minutes till the day is over is not the blessing of God. Come on, wise up! Go out there and get a life and make your dreams a reality.

## Martin Luther King

Martin Luther King was a dreamer. I am writing this chapter whilst in Alabama in the USA. Today I stood in one of the most famous pulpits in the world. I visited Dexter Avenue King Memorial Baptist Church in Montgomery, Alabama. This was the church where Martin Luther King Jnr. was the Pastor from 1954 until 1960. This was the place where the protest marches were organised after Rosa Parks refused to give up her seat on a bus. This was the pulpit where he delivered many of his heart-stirring sermons. This was the man responsible for one of the most passionate and inspirational speeches of all time, "I have a dream." I stood in that pulpit today and walked around the little church and was in awe of the world-changer who walked on that same floor and probably went over and over his sermons before mounting that small pulpit. How many times he would have said, "I can see the promised land." What a man, what a dream. He saw his land long before the assassin pulled the trigger. He dreamed of it and walked in it and brought others to it.

## Disney

Walt Disney was a dreamer. When his daughters were young he brought them to amusement parks and enjoyed the music and the rides as any young family would. He especially liked the carousel. He was captivated by the bright colours and music but, as the ride stopped, he saw the shabby horses and cracked paint and realised that his eyes had been fooled. He started to dream of a place where illusions would not be shattered and which gave the enjoyment of a park without the seedy side that accompanied many circuses and funfairs. His dream led eventually to Disneyland. *"If you can dream it, you can do it"*.

Two years ago we went, as a family, to Disney World in Florida. I still smile when I remember the rides and walking down the main street towards the castle. I recall how brilliant everything was, the tremendous attention to detail and the sheer fun of being there. For two wonderful weeks we walked the dream. Isaac, our youngest, loved the Buzz Lightyear ride and to be honest, we all did - we went back thirteen times! Cathy and I trying to outscore each other and making noises that adults were supposed to have stopped making after they left childhood, weren't they? Our children loved it but I think Mum and Dad were just as excited. That should not be a surprise as it was all carefully thought out by the massive Disney Corporation and Walt Disney in particular. The day we arrived would have been Walt Disney's 100th birthday.

## Josiah Spiers

Josiah Spiers was a dreamer. He was a children's evangelist at a time when children were not seen as mature enough to respond to the claims of the Gospel. Along with Thomas Bishop he formed the Children's Special Service Ministry (CSSM). In 1868, whilst on holiday in Llandudno, North Wales, he walked along the beach and saw children playing in the sand. He dreamt of preaching the gospel to them and so went and got some string and pebbles and helped them make texts in the sand. At the end of the week he invited their parents as well and shared the gospel with hundreds of people. It became the very first beach mission. Eventually CSSM evolved into Scripture Union which has been at the cutting edge of children's ministry for decades and also a major influence in my youth.

## Thomas Cook

Thomas Cook was a dreamer. He came to know the Lord and was a preacher as well as a businessman. He watched wealthy people go off on holiday and dreamt of making holidays affordable for the common working man. He started organising package holidays and the Thomas Cook travel firm was formed.

## Henry Ford

Henry Ford was a dreamer. He said, "the whole secret of a successful life is to find out what is one's destiny to do, and then do it." His dream was to create inexpensive mass-produced cars, to put them within the reach of the ordinary working person. In 1903 he formed the Ford Motor Company and started producing the Model T. In the first year they produced 6,000 but by the eighth year production went up to 500,000 and the price was brought down for the ordinary man.

The Bible inspires us to dream, to stretch further than we have been before. It encourages us to give up our small ambitions and reach for the sky. Look at a few verses:

Isaiah 54:2&3 "Enlarge the place of your tent, stretch your tent curtains wide, do not hold back; lengthen your cords, strengthen your stakes. For you will spread out to the right and to the left; your descendants will dispossess nations and settle in their desolate cities." What a promise, God wants us to expand and increase.

## The man called 'pain'

In the first book of Chronicles chapter 4 we read of Jabez, a young man whose name means 'pain'. I guess he got pretty fed up of people calling him that all the time and eventually he came before God and cried out to him, "Oh! that you would bless me and enlarge my territory! Let your hand be with me, and keep me from harm so that I will be free from pain"... and God granted his request. What a gracious God we have who sees and hears what we dream and cry out to him.

In Acts 6 we read about two deacons with enlarged ministries, Stephen (6:8) & Philip (8:6). They were called to wait on the tables and look after the needs of the widows etc. They did all that, but they had the desire to increase more and more. We read of them both preaching the gospel and Stephen losing his life for it, with Philip demonstrating the miraculous power of God.

**He was not confined by where his experience told him he could go**

They are inspiring stories and evidence of the power of the gospel, but later on in Acts 8:26 a very important preaching engagement needed to be attended to. Who would the council of heaven choose to lead this very important African to the Lord? This was the opening of the continent of Africa to the Gospel! God sent an angel to Philip to tell him that he was the man for the job. Why? Philip was a man with an enlarged heart who wanted more from God.

God knew that for an extraordinary assignment, He needed an extraordinary person and Philip fitted the bill. He was not confined by where his experience told him he could go, but he extended far beyond his natural restrictions, fulfilled God's mission and then travelled (or "was translated") in a way that was beyond the norm.

What about your land? Psalm 37 is all about our land and verse 4 tells us to delight ourselves in the Lord, who will give us the desires of our hearts. In other words, the land that God has for us is not some horrible calling that a sadistic god has dreamt up to punish us, or that a harsh god has formulated to discipline us. No! So long as our heart loves and is surrendered to God, our land is what we dream about, what excites us more than anything else can.

Your land could be much bigger than your experience so far. As you read the rest of this book, reflect on the land God has put in front of you. This is not for the faint-hearted; in fact, I believe that most miss it and settle for what they have already seen and tasted, content with being as comfortable as possible. They will be be just family-changers. But you have lifted this book because you are different. You are not merely a family-changer, you are a nation-changer, and God is expanding your capacity already. You are hungry for more, and God will satisfy you.

**Are you living your dream or are you simply living out someone else's dream?**

Take a moment to sit and think. Ask God to search your heart and help you to evaluate where you are. Do not allow the Devil to make you feel guilty. He is the Accuser and pushes down. God is the Challenger and lifts up. Ask Him to reveal His plans and purposes for your life and assess where you are today. Are you living your dream or are you simply living out someone else's dream? Are you heading somewhere? Have you a goal? Were there any dreams and ambitions you had as a younger Christian that time and circumstances have eroded from your heart? If they are gone and dead then let them stay there. But I have a feeling that many reading this book will start to feel those old dreams once again and that a work of restoration is starting to happen, that inside you are about to explode with vision and passion. I am excited whilst writing this as I have discovered by travelling to many places and talking to so many different people that there is a cry arising from the people of God. They are fed up of 'normal' living and long for the supernatural life, to see the miracles, to believe God for the impossible, to walk with God and experience His presence and approval as they serve Him each day. If this is you, read on!

## Chapter 2

# Joshua, the young man

In May 1982, I was called to the Principal's office in Cliff College, Derbyshire. I was to receive news that would change my life at that time. To be honest I thought I was going to be told off! One of my friends had skipped some of his classes and was gently reminded that it was not acceptable. I, too, had been a little flexible with my time that particular week and was expecting the same.

I was working in the college bookshop that afternoon, as I did regularly. During my second year I could not afford the fees so along with studying, I worked in the gardens or in the bookshop to help pay my way. My first year fees were paid for by my brother, Raymond. He was a hero to me. He joined the army at 16 as it was all he had ever wanted to do. At 21 he was brought into the SAS and served with them all over the world. He spent a lot of time in N. Ireland and we never knew when he would drop in to my parents' house in an unmarked car. It was a strange lifestyle and the sort of thing that we never discussed outside the family. Raymond just worked in England as far as anyone else was concerned. This was the reality of life in N. Ireland at that time. A wrong word could cost a life.

## The Falklands War

April 1982 saw the war in the Falklands. Mrs.Thatcher sent out the task force and it was on the minds and lips of everyone in England. Sitting in the TV room in Cliff, everyone had their opinions about war – some were for it, some against. What they did not know was that Raymond was already over there. My other brother, Wesley, had phoned me to tell me. So as everyone was debating, I did not care about the rights and wrongs, I just knew that my brother was there. The hard part was that I had to keep this to myself and so I prayed for him continually. I found out later that his group had retaken South Georgia, and Raymond himself had destroyed 11 Argentinian aircraft on Pebble Island, earning him the nickname 'Pucara Paddy'.

Dr. Skevington Wood called me into his study that afternoon and was very subdued. He asked me to sit down and said that he had some bad news for me, that my brother had been killed in a helicopter accident in the Falklands. 19 SAS men lost their lives that day, 19 of the best soldiers in the UK. I phoned my Dad in Enniskillen and he could not speak on the phone. I flew home immediately completely numb to what was happening. God came so close to me at that time and brought me and my family through it. Our house was the center of attention during that period as he was the first person from Ireland to lose their life in the war.

A year later in April 1983, My brother, Wesley, and I travelled with a group of the families and relatives to the Falkland Islands for a series of remembrance services for all those who lost their lives. We flew to Montevideo in Uruguay and sailed along the River Plait and down to the Islands. We were flanked by two warships and protected by the RAF. As the SAS helicopter was lost at sea, we flew out in a Hercules aircraft to the actual spot and circled over the water and dropped wreathes onto the sea. That was when it hit us as families; our loved ones were somewhere beneath.

## A recurring dream

For ten years after that time I had a recurring dream. I met up with Raymond in a variety of locations and it had all been a cover up. He was working undercover for the Government. That was why he had to be lost at sea; there could be no body. Then I would wake up in a sweat. These dreams only stopped after ten years.

Why am I recounting this story? Well, regardless of all that happened to Joseph, he said that God was in control (Genesis 50:20). God is not the author of bad things but He can use all things to work together for us. Indeed, He wants to use everything. I believe that nothing is wasted. I have been working as a Pastor for many years and, coming from N. Ireland where everyone goes to funerals, I am very well acquainted with what goes on. I know most of the funeral scriptures off by heart but it was only after Raymond died that I could truly identify with those who were bereaved. After that experience I knew what it was like to grieve. I knew what it was like to cry and mourn. The interesting thing is that other people could see that as well. People would open up to me because they knew I would understand.

The truth of the gospel is that God did not send a tract or a DVD from heaven; He sent his Son. Jesus was born as a vulnerable baby. He grew up as we did. He had the same burps, fell out of the same trees, and was tempted in the same way as we were and still are today. He appeared in a stable, travelled on a donkey, lived as a carpenter, preached all over the place with nowhere to lay his head. The truth is that he entered our world and because of that we can trust him.

**God did not send a tract or a DVD from heaven; He sent his Son**

People warm to folks who have been through what they have been through. Look at all the various charities; they are started generally by someone who has suffered in a particular way, and they attract people because they can identify with the founder.

So it is with us in the Christian life. All of us have been through circumstances, some good, some bad. But God does not label experiences as 'good' or 'bad'. He can use it all. Some of you reading this have been on drugs, some have had abortions, some in prison, some abused, others have lied and cheated, or been unfaithful. But you are where you are today by the grace of God. God has brought you through and He was there all the time. He did not cause all those bad things but He did know about them, and He is weaving them all in to His greater plan.

I was brought up in the Methodist Church and one of my favourite teachings from it is the doctrine of prevenient grace, or "the grace that comes before". I do not accept the idea of total depravity as we are all made in the image of God, so there is something in every person that reminds us of God. The idea of prevenient grace is beautiful. John Wesley thought of it long before we had the modern 'Engel scale' or 'sowing, reaping, keeping'. It says that God is leading every person to that place where they can find Him, where they can be born again. That God is at work in everyone, using circumstances and situations to bring them to Him. I love that. Every person has a history and whoever I meet today, God is already at work in their lives with the ultimate aim of them finding Christ.

## Nothing is wasted

The situations that I have been through and how I have responded to them can help someone else in their journey to God. So whatever you have been through or has happened to you, God can use, if you will allow Him to, to show someone else the road to God. Nothing is wasted.

In this first chapter, we are looking at how God has been working in the background in Joshua's life long before his 'call to ministry'. The question I want to ask is this, "What was God doing and teaching Joshua in each of these stories?" Joshua is a good character to throw these questions at because he is one of the few characters in the Bible to appear many times before his book.

So let us take a look at some of these passages where we read about Joshua.

## 1. The Battle of Rephidim

The first place that we encounter Joshua is in Exodus 17. We read from verse 8 that there is a battle against the Amalekites.

How important is Joshua in this story? I believe that if God repeats something in the Bible then it is for a reason. Therefore if you look at the words themselves, Joshua's name comes up regularly.

- In verse 9, Joshua chose the men.
- In verse 10, Joshua fought.
- In verse 13, Joshua overcame.

If we were there at that time and had a chat with Joshua on the night after this famous victory and asked him how he felt, I wonder what he would have said. He may have been a bit excited and proud of himself. After all, he chose the men, he fought and he overcame.

## Everybody is important

But then the men fought *with* him. I do not suppose that the men stood to one side while Joshua faced the enemy on his own. Also while Joshua was fighting, Moses was on top of the hill with the staff of God in his hand. Victory came as Moses held up his arms so he was also important. But then as Moses' arms were drooping, Aaron and Hur stepped in and supported the arms of Moses so they were also important. But from the viewpoint of Joshua, he might have been completely unaware of the guys on the hill.

I have done a lot of hill walking in Wales spending many a moment watching the boats from Conwy Mountain. I was aware that, although I could see them, it was very unlikely that they could see me. Also Joshua was in a fight. He did not pause the battle and get everyone to give his pal, Moses, a wave and then all hug and pose for a group photograph. So he may not have been aware that the battle was being won only when Moses' hands were held aloft. Here we see a team at work. Each one is important to the success of the mission.

**God has not called us to be supermen and superwomen**

It is the same with us in the land that the Lord is calling us to possess. God has not called us to be supermen and superwomen, He calls us into fellowship with others to stand alongside each other to get the job done.

Verse 14 is the most significant verse in the chapter. God asked Moses to write something on a scroll but to 'make sure that Joshua hears it'. Why was it so important that Joshua heard it? I believe that this was the first lesson in Joshua's training school. Joshua was completely unaware that one day God would call him to take over from Moses. He had no historical reason to assume it. He knew the stories of Abraham, Isaac and Jacob. He saw how God used the son to take over from the father. Moses was not his dad. But God knew He was preparing his man, who had many lessons to learn along the way.

So make sure that Joshua hears this: 'Jehovah Nissi' – the Lord is my Banner. I believe that God was teaching Joshua two things in this encounter:

Firstly, remember that there is teamwork involved in everything we attempt to do for the Lord. If Joshua can learn that at this stage of his life, then it will keep him from making the same mistakes as his predecessor, Moses. God had to send his father-in-law, Jethro, to show him how he needed to share the workload (Exodus 18).

## The Lord is our banner

Secondly, remember that the Lord is our banner. No matter how important individuals may seem to be, it is the Lord who will win the victory for us – He is in control. What a relief that should be to us. It will cause us to relax and realise that God will take care of us and it will stop us getting big-headed and full of ourselves. It all begins and ends with God. Jesus is described in the book of Hebrews as the Author and the Finisher of our faith. Without Him we are nothing, and with Him, He is the one who does the work and is still in control.

> LESSONS TO LEARN:
>
> TEAMWORK ✔
>
> GOD IS IN OVERALL CONTROL ✔

## 2. Up the mountain

The second passage is Exodus 24:13 where we see God emphasize something very simple yet profound. Joshua and Moses are up on the mountain of God and a significant expression here is repeated in several other places. Joshua is described as Moses' "servant", his "minister", or his "aide", depending on what version you are reading.

**Every person who God wants to use must start off as a servant to someone else's vision**

I believe that every person who God wants to use must start off as a servant to someone else's vision. There are many today who want the glory, the prestige and the big name, but that is not possible. God is not interested in sharing his glory with anyone else. We are servants, and before God will give us a vision of our own, He wants us to submit to the vision of another. That may be your local church and your Pastor.

In Matthew 8 a very important centurion came up to Jesus wanting him to heal his servant. When Jesus agreed to go with him, the centurion gives us amazing insight into how power and authority are delegated and given. Power comes through submission and this experienced and wise soldier knew that.

In Mark 10:43-45 we have the crazy account of James and John's request to Jesus. He has just told them that he is going to die and immediately they ask him if they can sit, one each side of him, in glory. How Jesus could have despaired at his thick disciples! He teaches them that, if anyone desires to have a great ministry, he must be the servant of all. But he goes on to that classic statement in verse 45 that even the Son of Man did not come to be served but to be a servant and give his life as a ransom for many.

LESSON TO LEARN:

WE ARE SERVANTS ✔

## 3. Into the tent

The third passage is in Exodus 33:7-11 and here we are getting to the heart of the man who God has chosen to follow Moses. Verse 7 tells us that Moses used to pitch his tent outside the camp. The language suggests that it was something he did on a regular basis. So this was a part of Moses' disciplined life. Joshua went with Moses into that tent. What was he doing? The Bible does not tell us and so we can only use our imaginations. Was Joshua involved in any way or did Moses simply ignore him and leave him in the corner? What was happening to Joshua as Moses conversed with God? Well, we can guess in an informed way because we read in verse 11 that when Moses left the tent, Joshua stayed there. Why would he do that?

## As a man speaks to his friend

Verse 11 also tells us that the Lord spoke to Moses as a man would speak to his friend. Wow! What does that mean? Well, I believe that you speak to your friend in a different way than you speak to anyone else. When I speak to people, sometimes I am careful what I say. Working in a church I need to be very careful – not everyone keeps confidences the way I would expect; not everyone can take a joke, etc. But with your friend, the masks come off. If your friend asks you how you are and you say, "Fine" instead of admitting that you have had a lousy day, then your friend will know immediately. That person knows you (warts and all) and still wants to be your friend. With a friend you can say things that are for that person's ears only, no pretence and lots of laughs. That is why he/she is your friend. I remember working with a pastor who liked to play squash and I played against him occasionally. If he had had a difficult pastoral situation or somebody in his congregation was giving him a hard time, he would name the ball after that person on that particular day. It was amazing how the guy enjoyed belting 'Sadie' up and down the squash court for an hour – it certainly seemed to relieve the stress and tension! But you can only share that sort of information with a friend. So I imagine that the Lord and Moses had a few laughs and shared a few frustrations about those miserable Israelites. No man had ever had the ear of God in this way. This was almost blasphemous. But Moses was glowing in the presence of God; so much so, they had to put a paper bag over his head when he left the tent!

## Joshua heard

Joshua heard and saw all of this. He was in a privileged position. As he watched from the corner something was happening in his heart also. Why did he stay in the tent after Moses left? I believe it was because he wanted to soak up some of the atmosphere. As he watched and listened, a real hunger was created inside his heart that one day he might commune with his God in that same way. Keep that in mind and turn to Joshua 1:5 where God tells Joshua that He will be with him in just the same way that He was with Moses. What a blessing that must have been for Joshua! The same way, the same sort of relationship, the same closeness, perhaps even the same familiarity. This might not have meant a lot to anyone else, but to Joshua it was the answer to the longing of his heart since the days when he sat at the feet of his master, Moses.

So Joshua stayed in the tent of meeting after Moses left. A successful leader is a servant who spends time with God. So what lesson was God teaching Joshua here in this tent?

He was learning how important it was to spend time with God, and to do so on a regular basis. Joshua was always there with Moses, so he was building both discipline and faithfulness into his life.

## How faithful are you?

I have been approached many times by people wanting to come with me on my preaching trips. Sometimes I take teams to various places, especially Africa. But the one thing I want to see in a person is how faithful they are in their local church. God has placed all of us within a family of believers (unless we are in a missionary situation where it is not possible) and that is where He will train us and get us to the place where He can use us. To be honest, if someone is sloppy in their church attendance and attitude to their local church leaders, then I have no reason to believe that they are not the same in their spiritual life. Therefore I assume that they are not the ideal person to take away on some preaching trip. God wants to build discipline and faithfulness into our characters long before the call to ministry will come. Remember Joshua still has no reason to believe that he will be the one to lead the children of Israel into the Promised Land, but God is watching and waiting.

> LESSONS TO LEARN:
>
> DISCIPLINE ✔
>
> FAITHFULNESS ✔

## 4. Back to school

The fourth passage in Numbers 11 involves some re-learning that Joshua needs to do. He has been in the Bible School of Moses for quite some time now and he is a very knowledgeable young man. Perhaps he knows too much and has already tried to put God into a box that God does not seem to fit.

This is another chapter where the Israelites are in complaining mode. They are fed up of manna and want some meat to eat. They complain again to Moses and Moses gets annoyed. He comes before God and says that he has had enough. But God tells Moses that the people will eat meat until they are sick of it. God explains that He has the power to do this and asks Moses to gather together the 70 Elders. They begin to prophesy but two of their number, Eldad and Medad are absent and miss out. But they also start prophesying in the camp where a young man sees them and runs to tell Moses. Joshua hears and pleads with Moses to stop them, as they are not doing it right. He is reminding Moses that there is a proper way to do things and Joshua knows what that way is. In verse 28 Joshua is concerned about order and asks Moses to restore some order, but Moses tells him off.

### Mission surprise

I remember as a young man of 17, going on a mission to Dublin whilst working with the Methodist Church in Ireland on their Youth Evangelism Team. We had a full programme and on one particular day we were supposed to visit the Methodist College. This did not materialize and we went into a Roman Catholic school instead. Now I spent most of my childhood growing up in a Protestant environment in Enniskillen in the North of Ireland so this was a new experience for me. However what an opportunity to share the real gospel to people who, in my opinion, had probably not heard it before. Well, we went in during lunchtime and did some drama, songs and speaking. The place was packed to the doors and the priest came to see us immediately afterwards. He shook our hands so hard with a massive beam on his face and said how wonderful it was – I went into shock!

## A true worshipper

During my time at Cliff College I was asked to go and speak at a church near Manchester. I had been invited by a friend who was studying at a music college and the worship was led by her colleagues from the Christian Union. It was an incredible live worship experience with an orchestra. One of her friends shone above the others. This young man had such an apparent love for the Lord; he was enthusiastic in his worship and in his conversation and, as we were chatting afterwards, I asked him what Fellowship he attended and he told me he went to the Catholic Church. Again it came as a bit of a shock.

I am writing this, not as an advertising campaign for the Roman Catholic Church, as my mind sees so many things in that system that I feel are wrong, but as an example of how I, as a young man, had everything sewn up and worked out until I was confronted by something I could not understand. Joshua, too, had it in his mind that there was a right way and a wrong way. In many cases that is true. But here Moses speaks up and questions his reasoning and motives and says, "Let God be God!"

**If we continue to do what we have always done, we should not be surprised if we get the same results that we have always had**

Sometimes God might desire to move in ways we don't think He should. Let us keep an open mind. It has often been said that if we continue to do what we have always done, we should not be surprised if we get the same results that we have always had. If we are in the midst of a revival, then keep on, but sometimes we need to open our minds and explore new ways and avenues to reach people for God. We live in a society that desperately needs God. His love for them far exceeds our love, so we should not be surprised if He uses whatever ways He can to reach them.

What is God teaching Joshua here? A willingness to change. We do not like change. We are creatures of habit; we do the same things each week. Even on Sunday we run our church programmes in a certain way. If we come from a traditional church we may follow through what the 'free-er' churches sometimes call a 'hymn sandwich', often a short affair with a collection of old and new, but very similar Sunday by Sunday. The 'free-er' churches have their own format, ('led by the Spirit' of course), but the same each week. It is usually lively worship followed by quieter worship followed by the Word. It is certainly not a sandwich, more like a Big Mac, a long time to wait, an awful lot of filling and not a lot of meat. We sit in the same place each week, dress in the same way, talk to the same people and so on. Sometimes there is the person who will interrupt the proceedings with 'a word from the Lord' or a prayer and when this is from God, wow! But when it is not, then we get into a mess and the Service becomes a playground for the weird and wonderful!

## Shopping!

I am a man of habit. Some habits are good, some are bad. Cathy and I like to go shopping at the Metro Centre, one of the largest shopping malls in Europe. It is very big with thousands of car parking spaces. The problem is that I have to park in the same spot every time. Do not ask me why, but my car just automatically drives me into the yellow quadrant and onto the third floor of the car park. It is either satellite navigation or perhaps divine guidance but I cannot park anywhere else. If I do, I go into a blind panic, I cannot find anything and my day can be ruined by such a tragedy! It got so bad for a while that if I was on the wrong road then I did a U-turn in the middle of the road to get to the right place. I expect you are thinking that I am making this up, but I kid you not. I admit it, it is very sad and a bit pathetic, but it is an exaggerated version of what we all do every day. We have our little schedules and they usually run on a regular cycle, washing on Monday, swim on Tuesday, shopping on Friday and so on.

God showed Joshua that he needed to be flexible and willing to change to allow God to do whatever He so desired to do, in whatever way He wanted to do it.

> LESSONS TO LEARN:
>
> OPENNESS TO CHANGE ✔
>
> FLEXIBILITY ✔

### 5. Into Canaan

In Numbers 13 God told Moses to send spies into the land of Canaan to see what the land was like. Did God not already know? Had He never been there? No, God knew what it was like; this exercise was for the people. From verses 17-20, we read that Moses asked them to be truthful. He was not asking for an overly positive report, just an accurate description of what God's promised land was like. This was not an exercise in blind faith, rather one of true analysis. There were twelve spies, one from each of the tribes. Joshua, whose name means 'Jehovah is salvation', the equivalent of 'Jesus', and Caleb, whose name means

**This was not an exercise in blind faith, rather one of true analysis**

'boldness', are both significant here. Names were so important in Bible days and I think that any church that has a combination of Joshuas and Calebs will be blessed. Joshua will hear God and say we need to have an open air sometime; Caleb will come in and say that the bus is running now, jump in!

The twelve go into the land and come back with the report and, true enough, it does flow with milk and honey and grapes. It is a fantastic place, but there are also giants there. So the ten give this analysis with special emphasis on the size of the enemy.

## A statement of faith

Caleb jumps up in verse 30 to silence them and says that they can take the land. This was a statement of faith based on what he had seen and also what the word of the Lord had said. Unfortunately what the ten say next is based on what they had seen and their own imaginations. They gave their conclusion right at the beginning: "We are not able to do it". In verses 31 to 33 they explain why they have come to that conclusion, which is based it on the following assumptions.

1. the people of Canaan are too strong
2. the land devours those living in it
3. the Israelites are only like grasshoppers

In fact they said that they looked like grasshoppers in the Canaanites' eyes. How could they know that? Do you think for one moment that they had a survey and stopped people along the road and asked them to tick a box: What do you think the Israelites look like? (a) grasshoppers (b) mice (c) elephants (d) donkeys? No, this was sheer imagination at work.

But then we have one of the most frightening verses in the whole Bible. Numbers 14:2. The Israelites grumbled and said, "If only we had died in Egypt! Or in this desert!" Why a frightening verse? Well, later in the chapter, in verses 28-29, God said that He had heard their grumbling and taken note of their request and would do the very things that He heard them say – if they wanted to die in the desert, then fine. That is exactly what happened. An entire generation except Joshua and Caleb perished in the wilderness. What a waste! This frightens me to the point where I say to God, "Please help me never to say something so daft that it will disqualify me from the incredible plan you have for my life." David put this another way in Psalm 141:3 – "Set a guard over my mouth, O LORD; keep watch over the door of my lips".

## A different spirit

In verses 6-9, we see a different spirit working in Joshua and Caleb. They knew that they could take the land if the Lord was with them and pleased with them. They try to turn the attention of the people back to God to see that He is with them and has given the land to them. Note how many times in these verses that 'The Lord' is mentioned. 'If the Lord delights in us', 'He will bring us in', 'Do not rebel against the Lord', ' The Lord is with us'. But the people talked of stoning them. So God condemned them to wander in the desert for 40 years, one year for each day the spies explored the land of Canaan.

With the help of Caleb, God had taught another important lesson to Joshua; to have the eyes of faith and see the potential of what can happen with God. We need to learn from this if we want God to use us in our particular job or ministry. There are plenty of people who will tell you many reasons why the job cannot be done, but there might only be one Caleb who can encourage you to go ahead and do it. Champions are those who know which voice to listen to.

**Champions are those who know which voice they should listen to**

There are times when we need to silence the voices, tune into God, then go ahead and obey Him. I am sure that you can think of many reasons why you could get discouraged today when you think of what your land might be. I am sure that you can come up with a few giants. They may be financial ones, circumstantial ones and a host of others. As these giants face you as you look into the land, ask the same questions Moses asked. What is the land like? Has God really given it to me? Is it worth taking a risk for? Then get your boots on, grab hold of your rifle, jump out of the truck and go for it! You will never know unless you try; and the worst you can do is fail – and at least then the Lord knows He has found a servant who is willing to do whatever He asks; and that is all He is looking for.

LESSONS TO LEARN:

SEE THE POSSIBLE ✔

DWELL ON THE GOOD ✔

## 6. Into leadership

In Numbers 27:15ff Moses asks the Lord to choose a man to succeed him, to be a shepherd for the sheep. I guess he must have imagined that it would be Joshua and indeed Moses may well have had a tremendous shock if the Lord had suggested anyone else. But God did ask Moses to take Joshua, a man in whom is the Spirit (vs.18) and lay hands on him. God told Moses to give Joshua some of his authority. Now Joshua is beginning to see that the Lord has been moulding him and preparing him for this particular day.

We see similar instructions in Deuteronomy 1:38. Moses would only see the land from a distance; he was not going to set foot in it, not yet anyhow. So God told Moses to encourage Joshua because this man would enter the land and cause Israel to inherit it. The same thought is in Deuteronomy 3:28 where Moses was told to encourage and strengthen Joshua, for he would cause the people to inherit the land.

Then in Deuteronomy 31:7 Moses is giving one of his last speeches to the people telling them that Joshua is to be the one that will lead them into the Promised Land; he will cause them to take the land. God was teaching Joshua to use authority before the day when he really needed it.

> LESSON TO LEARN:
>
> HOW TO USE AUTHORITY ✔

And so the scene was set; God was shaping Joshua's life long before He actually called him into the ministry. That will come soon enough. God has it all in control and so it is in your life. David says, in Psalm 139, that all the days ordained for us were written in God's book before one of them came to be.

God knows what He is doing in your life. He is preparing something wonderful for you. I suspect that it is much bigger than that which you have seen up until now. Get ready for a new move!

# Chapter 3

# Moses, my servant, is dead

I guess you could call Joshua 1 the call of Joshua, although, as we have seen, this is not the start. However, it is the call, just as in Jeremiah 1 we read the call of Jeremiah and in Isaiah 6 we read the call of Isaiah. Here God is commissioning the young man, Joshua, for the task that He has been preparing him for all his life. For now, anyway, the training is over. There comes a time when the preparation for tomorrow must stop and tomorrow becomes today. Training must have a goal and here we have it for Joshua in Joshua 1:1-5.

**There comes a time when the preparation for tomorrow must stop and tomorrow becomes today**

*"After the death of Moses the servant of the Lord, the Lord said to Joshua son of Nun, Moses' assistant: "Moses my servant is dead. Now then, you and all these people, get ready to cross the Jordan river into the land I am about to*

*give to them – to the Israelites. I will give you every place where you set your foot, as I promised Moses. Your territory will extend from the desert to Lebanon, and from the great river, the Euphrates – all the Hittite country – to the Great Sea on the west. No-one will be able to stand up against you all the days of your life. As I was with Moses, so I will be with you; I will never leave you nor forsake you.*

## 1. No redundant Christians

*'After the death'*

God waited until Moses was dead before He called Joshua. Why did He do that? Was it out of respect to Moses, to avoid hurting his feelings? I believe that it was because God used Moses right up until the day of his death. He died at just the right time, not a day too early or a day too late. You see, there are no redundancies in the Kingdom. God does not pay a person off and retire them to some home where they can sit collecting dust until their number is up.

We see an example of this with David in Acts 13:36; it was only after David had served God in his own generation that he fell asleep or died. In other words, God used him right up until He called him home.

The Bible says in Proverbs 29:18, that without a vision, people perish. I have seen that happen many times. It can happen when a man retires after a life of work. He has faithfully served up to age 65 and then has nothing to do. He has made no plans and so the boredom kills him. I have seen it happen numerous times in Old People's Homes where everything is done for the folks there. It is wonderful that we have such caring places. But many of these folk were used to making all their own decisions, where to go, shop, holiday, when to go to bed, what to have for their tea. Many of these decisions are now made for them so they start to deteriorate.

You see, without a vision, people perish. We all need a reason to be alive. We need purpose and something to get out of bed for each morning. So if you have breath in your lungs today, then God still has purpose and vision for your life. When you get to the end, He will take you home.

## 2. Still a servant

*'Moses, the servant of the Lord'*

Moses, as we have seen, was one of the most dynamic characters in all of history and the one who communed with God face to face. Yet here he is described as a servant of the Lord. It does not matter how far we go or how high we climb, we will never outgrow servanthood. Our Master and greatest example, the Lord Jesus Christ, was servant as well as King.

We see a lovely picture of this humility in John 13 where John tells us that Jesus was acutely aware that his hour had come and he was soon going to die. The devil had convinced Judas to betray Jesus, but Jesus knew that all things were in his hands. With this backdrop we see him take a towel and begin to wash his disciples' feet, telling his disciples that they also should wash each other's feet.

## 3. Don't mock the past

*'Moses, my servant'*

When I first moved to England in 1999, I used to travel around the UK preaching in various churches. Some places I went to only once, several of which were in London. I remember going to one big fellowship in the centre of London on a Sunday afternoon. It was a Pentecostal church and I sat in the congregation for the first part of the service. When it was my turn to preach, I was given a long introduction by the Pastor who must have asked me pertinent questions before the service began – I do not really remember. However I do remember the introduction. It lasted quite a long time being my first visit there. It went something like this:

> **"This afternoon, we have the privilege, no the honour, to have the man of God in our midst** (loud cheers and applause); **this man has travelled the world preaching the gospel** (more loud applause and whistles – I did not realise that my one trip to Majorca had been so widely advertised!); **This Apostle of God** (more hallelujahs) **used to be a Methodist** (cries of derision and disbelief, mixed with "Lord, have mercy") **but now he's a Pentecostal** (then the roof came off, hallulajahs, line dancing, river dancing, Glory to God everywhere). (It was going well so far, but then he really spoiled it). **Today I want to**

**present to you the man of God, the Reverend BEN KINGSLEY!"**

Well the place went mad; not only was I a globe-trotting evangelist who had seen the light and rejected his old Methodist roots, but now I was completely bald and had played the leading role in 'Ghandi'! Well, I had to laugh, but I do not remember a thing about that meeting apart from the introduction. My point is serious though. We are tremendously privileged to be alive and serving God today. Many reading this book will be living in a free country where there are few restrictions on serving God. Many in the past gave their lives for us to enjoy such a blessing.

In Hebrews chapter 11 we read about the great heroes of the faith. Many of them gave their lives for what they believed. We are surrounded by that great cloud of witnesses and so Hebrews chapter 12 exhorts us to run the race marked out before us.

## The Relay Race

I love watching athletics on TV. I look forward to the Olympics and the Commonwealth Games which come to their climax with the relay races. There has been tremendous rivalry over the years between the British and the Americans and although America seems to dominate the individual sprints, Britain tends to shine in the relays. The 4 x 100m relay is perhaps the most exciting race of the games. All the sprinters will be sub-10 second runners, so the speed is not the most crucial. The race is won or lost in the baton changes. They practice this again and again until they get it right. When the race is eventually won, the credit will go to the whole team. The race is not over until the last one has crossed the line. There have been many runners in the Christian race, but it is our turn now and we have to give it our best shot. I am grateful for those who ran a good race before me. God said to Joshua, "Moses was my servant". Do not mock him, he prepared the way for where you want to go.

I was brought up in the Methodist Church and I thank God for it. It was there that I first found the Lord; there that I was nurtured by so many godly ministers; in its Bible College that I discovered more about the Holy Spirit, and there that the call to serve God came very strongly into my life. I will never speak against it; I was handed a good baton from it. I remember one of my ministers, the Rev. George Good, being such a godly man, was a real model of God for me. I remember at Cliff College the Rev. Skevington Wood, a more holy man I have yet to meet. They ran a good race and now I have the baton.

## International Gospel Outreach

Serving as a minister with International Gospel Outreach has been a blessing in my life. God led me into it and I praise God for it. Many of the members have been so encouraging to me over the years. When David Greenow handed the baton over to me several years ago, what a race he had run. His leg of that particular race was over and he is still there watching as I give the race my best shot.

Working in New Life Baptist Church, Northallerton has also been a real joy in my life. I had the privilege of working alongside Pastor George Breckon. I do not know if I will ever again meet a person with such a love and compassion for lost people. What a race he ran and what an inspiration he was to those of us waiting in the wings.

Never mock the past. You may do things a little differently but that is fine. God allowed you and I to be alive in this day and age and it is our turn to run now.

Sometimes it is good to consider what the Lord has done in our lives and to say thanks. He tells us in Deuteronomy 8:10-14 to remember how God has delivered us. In the New Testament Jesus set before us the bread and the wine as a remembrance of him (1 Corinthians 11:24).

But that is not the end of the story.

## 4. Don't let the past intimidate you

*"Moses, my servant, is dead"*

Moses was fantastic but his job is done, you're my man now. God was telling Joshua that he must not be intimidated by Moses. Moses was a fantastic leader and it must have been an awesome thought to be taking over from him, but God had taken him home and it was Joshua's turn.

Many times we can allow the past to stop us giving our best for the future. The past's problems, inadequacies or victories can hinder us. We can say that it could never be this good again, or that we failed in the past, therefore we will fail again.

**Many times we can allow the past to stop us giving our best for the future**

Paul wrote to Timothy in 2 Timothy 4:7, *"I have fought the good fight, I have finished the race, I have kept the faith."* He has recognised that the baton change in the relay race is in sight and it is Timothy's turn now. In 2 Timothy 1:6 Paul encourages him to fan into flame God's gift. There are many examples of intimidated people throughout the Scriptures:

- ❖ In Exodus 3:11 when God called the great Moses he replied, "Who am I?"
- ❖ When God called Gideon in Judges 6:15, he answered "I am from a weak family."
- ❖ When God called Jeremiah in Jeremiah 1:6, he responded, "I am just a child!"

We all have good reasons why we could and should feel intimidated, but God is the One who has called us, and if He has called us then He is the One who will equip us.

I used to hear people say, "We need John Wesley back today", or "We need another Smith Wigglesworth". Certainly they were great men of God, but they were God's men in the right place at the right time. If God had wanted them around today, they would be here. The truth is that these men are dead and it is your turn now.

## 5. So many lives depend on what you do

*'YOU and all these people ...'*

Joshua would lead the people into the land of faith. He would cause them to inherit it. In other words his ministry did not exist on its own, he was responsible for the whole lot. What a load to carry! Their future depended on him. The decisions that he would make would have an influence on those who followed. He was being watched all the time. What a responsibility!

I have been so aware of this over the years. In my ministry to this point I have worked a lot with young people. I did not choose to be a role model but am one nevertheless. It is the same with you. If you are in ministry, then your congregation is watching you. Your neighbours are watching you. Only a fool would say that it does not matter how I behave and what I do. No, many lives depend on what you do.

We used to sing that old song a lot:

*'I'm going on, I'm going on,*
*I'm going on towards the mark,*
*towards my home.*
*So many lives depend on what I do;*
*Give me the strength, O Lord,*
*I'm going on with you.'*

Your response to situations of pressure, the places you go, the films you watch, the things you drink, the language you use, the way you treat your family and other people, the way you use your time etc. etc. People are watching and, whether you like it or not, some people will use you as a standard. I am answerable for that. That's why I made a commitment to the Lord as a teenager that I would not drink alcohol. It is one of the biggest problems in our culture today. Now you can drink all you like till the cows come home, but you can never point the finger at me and say it was because of my example!

## People are watching

I might have lost a few of you right there, but I want you to come with me further. Some of these things are seen as negative and in terms of what we do not do. There is something far more important than that. People are watching us to see the sorts of steps of faith that we are willing to make. So if I, as a Christian leader, fail to walk by faith, then I cannot make any demands on someone else to walk by faith. If a Pastor in a church has never taken a risk then he or she will never produce people in their congregation who will take risks. It stands to reason. We cannot produce fruit from a seed we have not sown. Now stop right here and take note of this; there are people today waiting to do some amazing things for God, but they seem unable to move until you do your amazing thing. Their step of faith is dependent on your step of faith. They are waiting and watching for you to step out of your boat and walk on the water. You are a leader of men and nations if you choose to believe what the Scripture says about you. You do not have to do it. However by not taking your steps of faith, you are robbing and selling short all those others who look up to you as their role model. Joshua had to take these people across the Jordan, there was far more at stake than just his future. The whole direction of the nation hung in the balance as he moved forward. I feel this so strongly that it has encouraged me not to hold back in trusting God. It is one of the reasons that we, as a family, have taken the steps we have over the past few years.

People see how we act and respond to the call of God; they see us in church and on Monday morning. They see how important the Word of God is in our lives. They see the way we spend our money and the time we have for people. So many lives depend on what we do.

## 6. Every place you set your foot

*'Cross the Jordan ... I will give you every place where you set your foot'*

I have often thought of this scenario. God tells Joshua to go across the river but, like all of us, I guess, he would have preferred to have a little more concrete guidance. God reveals to him that He has given him 'wherever he puts his foot'. This is very important in the walk of faith. Sometimes we want every little step written and marked on a roadmap to carry along with us. I sometimes imagine Joshua, having crossed the Jordan, standing on the river bank on one leg seeking God for the right place to put his foot down. What if he puts it in the wrong place? What if he turned right when God really wanted him to turn left? What a problem! You know, as ridiculous as it sounds, that is exactly what many Christians do today. They feel that the Lord is guiding in a certain direction, they have had the nudge, but they want more and are afraid to go in that way in case it is the wrong way. Well, I have news for you. For Joshua, both ways were right. Why? Because God told him that He would give him *every place* where he set his foot.

**For Joshua, both ways were right**

Here we see the combination of faith and action. We take a step believing that it is the will of God and we go for it. Later on in this book, I will show you how you can know the will of God for you, without doubt.

I admire William Carey. He is the one who made famous the phrase "Expect great things from God, attempt great things for God." He is sometimes called the Father and Founder of modern missions. But it was while listening to others beseeching God to save the heathen, observing that no-one actually went to tell the heathen about Christ, that he spoke the above phrase. He perceived that there needed to be the two things working in tandem. We need the faith and the belief for sure, but if it is not matched with the willingness to go and do something about it then it is worthless.

God said to Joshua that He had given him everywhere that he placed his foot. This is exemplified later on through

Caleb in Joshua 14:10-12 "Give me this mountain". Caleb was 40 years old when he and Joshua explored the land of Canaan. Now 45 years later, at the age of 85, he is still bold and walking by faith.

Joshua needed to know that God would give him everywhere he placed his feet, as later on he would have to put it into practice big time. In chapter 6 he is approaching Jericho and God tells him to march around the city. So he needed to have confidence in what God had said to him. Hebrews 11:30 tells us that by faith Jericho's walls fell.

### 7. Massive Territory

*'Your territory will extend ...'*
The devil will tell you what you cannot do but the Lord will tell you what you can do. God emphasizes the magnitude. This is a big place that God has provided for them. It will have everything that they could possibly need.

God is in the encouraging business; He always tells us that we can do it, just as a father will cheer his child on. God is in the extending business. He sees the future for us, he made us the way we are and therefore knows exactly what we are capable of. He wants us to look up and see the size of the plan.

### 8. No one will stand against you

*'... All the days of your life'*
What a promise! Joshua would be guaranteed success for ever. We read in Isaiah 54:17 'No weapon that is formed

against you shall prosper' and in 2 Corinthians 2:14 'But thanks be to God, who always leads us in triumphal procession in Christ and through us spreads everywhere the fragrance of the knowledge of him'. God has promised victory, and we know that Jesus secured the victory on the cross. We are promised that we will succeed – not only for today but all the days of our life. What wonderful security!

All this is tremendous reassurance for Joshua. He is successor to the greatest hero, which must have been a daunting task, but here God is encouraging him to get out there and do it and he will succeed.

No man will be able to stand against him. This is important, as we are all aware of the enemy in our lives. We seek to have on the full armour of God and resist him. But when the enemy has a human face it is perhaps more difficult. God assures Joshua that no man will be able to defeat him. We will be looking at the topic of fear at a later stage, but here I want you to consider what the Bible has to say about one particular fear, the fear of man.

❖ Proverbs 29:25 tells us that the fear of man will prove to be a snare, but whoever trusts in the Lord is kept safe. Hence the only way to be free from the fear of man is to trust in the Lord.

❖ In John 7:13 Jesus went up to Jerusalem for the Feast of Tabernacles. People were discussing him before he arrived and they were very divided in their opinions.

Many folk recognised the good that he had done and some believed that he was the Messiah, but verse 13 states that no-one would say anything for fear of the Jews. Fear of man kept them silent, and the fear of man has the ability to keep our tongues from saying what we know to be the truth.

❖ In John 9 we have the account of Jesus healing the man who had been blind from birth. It was a beautiful miracle that brought a whole new world of colour into the man's life. Some Jews came to his parents throwing doubt on the miracle by saying he was not really born blind and so questioned his parents. Verse 22 says that fear of the Jews kept the parents from saying anything. Is that not amazing? The power of fear!

❖ John 12:42-43 is even worse. Many believed in Jesus but would not confess him because they were afraid of being thrown out of the Synagogue. What follows is a terrifying indictment on them. Verse 43 declares that they loved praise from men more than praise from God. Let it be your prayer that such a statement could never be said of you. We all need to be sure that we live in reverential fear of the Almighty God and that what people think is really unimportant in the larger scheme of things.

❖ Luke 23:23 is one of the saddest verses in the Bible. As you read through the account of Jesus before Pilate a picture emerges of a leader who really wants to let

Jesus go, especially after his wife warns him about the dream she has had. Pilate tries his best to release him but eventually he gives in to the cries of the people. Pilate changed his plans because he was afraid of the people, and we have the frightening phrase, 'their shouts prevailed.' Fear of man can change the mind of a man who was convinced of the way he should go.

- In Jeremiah 1:17 God gives it straight to Jeremiah. He has a choice: either go and speak and not be afraid, or God will terrify him before the people. Fear of man is not an option for us, it will be a continual snare to us if we give in to its pressure.

But God has given us the antidote; trust in the Lord and we shall escape that snare (Proverbs 29:25). God promised Joshua that no man would be able to stand before him or speak against him or prevail over him all the days of his life. Confess that promise today and make it your own!

## 9. We are never abandoned

*'I will never leave you or forsake you..'*
God is giving Joshua a guarantee that He will stay with him always and never abandon him. So Joshua can relax; God will look after him. So with us; we are promised by Jesus in Matthew 28:20 that he would be with us always, even to the end.

Hebrews 13:5-6 says 'God has said, "Never will I leave you; never will I forsake you." So we say with confidence,

"The Lord is my helper; I will not be afraid. What can man do to me?"' This is a beautiful verse that is a spoken response to the words of God. He has said that He will not leave us. That is wonderful, but it demands a spoken response from us also, and I encourage you to say this when you feel afraid, or you are driving in your car on a dangerous road, or you are all alone: "The Lord is my helper; I will not be afraid. What can man do to me?"

## The presence of the Lord

We need to rediscover an awareness of the presence of the Lord. I was in the USA recently conducting a wedding for some friends of mine when, afterwards, at the reception, a man approached me and started talking. He wanted to know if I was reformed. Well, at first I wanted to say that I used to chew gum or used to pester my teachers but now I am a reformed character. However I knew that he was trying to pull me into a big theological debate about predestination, eternal salvation and other things, and I did not want to go there.

Then before speaking in some other churches I was quizzed by the Pastor about what I was and what I believed. Was I a Pentecostal or what? I understand that a Pastor has to be very wary and careful who he allows into his pulpit, but it started me on an investigation to find myself and who I really was. You see, I am not in a Methodist church any longer so I guess I am not really a Methodist; I worship at a Baptist church but I am not really a Baptist; indeed I used to call myself a Methodist missionary to the Baptists! I preach in many Pentecostal churches but I do not know if I am one of them either. Cathy was saved in the Salvation Army but she is not a Salvationist; she attended an Anglican church but she is not an Anglican. So what are we? I went for a long walk one morning and spent some time with the Lord and He showed me exactly what I am and what makes me what I am. I discovered that I am simply a child of God and what makes me different is that His Presence is with me.

When God said to Joshua that He would always be with him, it was the best news Joshua would ever hear. I looked up some Scriptures that talked about the presence of God and they are a blessing. It is the one thing that marks out the people of God as different. Look at the following characters and how they relate to the presence of God:

1. **WE MUST ACCEPT IT AS A FACT**

*Gideon: Judges 6:12.*
When the angel of the LORD appeared to Gideon, he said, "**The LORD is with you**, mighty warrior." So we have to accept it as a fact. Gideon did not feel that God was with him, but that did not change the fact that He was.

*Jacob: Genesis 28:16-17.*
When Jacob awoke from his sleep, he thought, "Surely **the LORD is in this place**, and I was not aware of it." Jacob was not aware that God was there.

## 2. IT BRINGS SIGNIFICANCE TO OUR LIVES

*Samuel: 1 Samuel 3:19.*
**The LORD was with Samuel** as he grew up, and he let none of his words fall to the ground.
*David: 1 Samuel 18:12.*
Saul was afraid of David, because **the LORD was with David** but had left Saul. In everything he did he had great success, because **the LORD was with him**.

*Mary, the mother of Jesus: Luke 1:28.*
The angel went to her and said, "Greetings, you who are highly favored! **The Lord is with you**."
Matthew 1:23 The virgin will be with child and will give birth to a son, and they will call him Immanuel – which means, **"God with us."**

## 3. IT BRINGS BLESSING

*Joseph: Genesis 39:2-3.*
The LORD was with Joseph and he prospered, and he lived in the house of his Egyptian master. When his master saw that **the LORD was with him** and that the LORD gave him success in everything he did, Joseph found favour in his eyes and became his attendant.

*Saul: 1 Samuel 10:7.*
Once these signs are fulfilled, do whatever your hand finds to do, for **God is with you**.

## 4. IT BRINGS POWER

*Jesus: Acts 10:38.*
... how God anointed Jesus of Nazareth with the Holy Spirit and power, and how he went around doing good and healing all who were under the power of the devil, because **God was with him**.

## 5. IT BRINGS ENDURANCE

*Isaiah 43:1-2.*
But now, this is what the LORD says – he who created you, O Jacob, he who formed you, O Israel: "Fear not, for I have redeemed you; I have summoned you by name; you are mine. When you pass through the waters**, I will be with you**; and when you pass through the rivers, they will not sweep over you. When you walk through the fire, you will not be burned; the flames will not set you ablaze.

*Psalm 23:4.*
Even though I walk through the valley of the shadow of death, I will fear no evil, **for you are with me**; your rod and your staff, they comfort me.

## 6. IT BRINGS PROOF

*Isaac: Genesis 26:28.*
They answered, "We saw clearly that **the LORD was with you**; so we said, 'There ought to be a sworn agreement between us and you'. Let us make a treaty with you.

*Shadrach, Mashach & Abednego: Daniel 3:24-26.*
Then King Nebuchadnezzar leaped to his feet in amazement and asked his advisers, "Weren't there three men that we tied up and threw into the fire?" They replied, "Certainly, O King." He said, "Look! **I see four men** walking around in the fire, unbound and unharmed, and the fourth looks like a son of the gods." Nebuchadnezzar then approached the opening of the blazing furnace and shouted, "Shadrach, Meshach and Abednego, servants of the Most High God, come out! Come here!" So Shadrach, Meshach and Abednego came out of the fire.

*The early disciples: Acts 11:21.*
**The Lord's hand was with them**, and a great number of people believed and turned to the Lord.

## 7. IT BRINGS INTIMACY

*Moses: Exodus 33:12-17.*
Moses said to the LORD, "You have been telling me, 'Lead these people,' but you have not let me know whom you will send with me. You have said, 'I know you by name and you have found favour with me.' If you are pleased with me, teach me your ways so I may know you and continue to find favour with you. Remember that this nation is your people." The LORD replied, **"My Presence will go with you**, and I will give you rest."
Then Moses said to him, **"If your Presence does not go with us, do not send us up from here**. How will anyone know that you are pleased with me and with your people

unless you go with us? What else will distinguish me and your people from all the other people on the face of the earth?" And the LORD said to Moses, "I will do the very thing you have asked, because I am pleased with you and I know you by name."

*Acts 4:13.*
When they saw the courage of Peter and John and realized that they were unschooled, ordinary men, they were astonished and they took note that **these men had been with Jesus.**

**8. IT BRINGS ANTICIPATION OF HEAVEN**
*John 14:3.*
And if I go and prepare a place for you, I will come back and take you to be with me, that **you also may be where I am.**

*Ezekiel 48:35.*
"The distance all around will be 18,000 cubits. "And the name of the city from that time on will be: **THE LORD IS THERE.**"

This is the greatest blessing that we have as the children of God. God created us so that we could be with Him. In the great plan of salvation, Jesus came as our Emmanuel, God with us. He is preparing a place for us so that we can be with him. What a wonderful thing to know the presence of the Lord in our lives day by day. You are not on your own, God is with you!

So God is calling Joshua and the time is now. The moment comes in all our lives when we need to extend ourselves and launch out into something new in God. We cannot train forever.

Moses left a fine example, but it was Joshua's turn now. Jesus started and finished a work when he came and died and rose again but he sends us out.
John 20:21 says, "as the Father has sent me so I send you."

We have had great examples throughout history but they are all gone now. They have left a great legacy and have smoothed out the road ready for us to come along. I do not know about you, but I do know about me. I am ready, the training is done, my kit is on, my feet are on the blocks and I am ready to go!

## Chapter 4

# Be strong and courageous

What an awesome land lies in front of Joshua. He is taking over from Moses and that seems a daunting task. But if the children of Israel did not always obey Moses, are they likely to obey Joshua? He has been instructed to cause them to inherit the land. God is well aware of what it is going to take to lead millions of people into places that they may not always want to go. So God tells Joshua to be strong and courageous; and just in case he did not hear it the first time, He repeats it another two times. Indeed Moses had already said it to Joshua in Deuteronomy 31:7, "Be strong and courageous, for you must go with this people into the land that the LORD swore to their forefathers to give them, and you must divide it among them as their inheritance."

God does not repeat words for no reason. There are three distinct guidelines that He wants Joshua to follow. He wants him to be strong and courageous because of what is facing Joshua. He shows him why and how he can be strong.

Joshua 1:6-9.
*"Be strong and courageous, because you will lead these people to inherit the land I swore to their forefathers to give them.*
*Be strong and very courageous. Be careful to obey all the law my servant Moses gave you; do not turn from it to the right or or the left, that you may be successful wherever you go.*
*Do not let this Book of the Law depart from your mouth; meditate on it day and night, so that you may be careful to do everything written in it. Then you will be prosperous and successful.*
*Have I not commanded you? Be strong and courageous. Do not be terrified; do not be discouraged, for the LORD your God will be with you wherever you go."*

Three times God said to Joshua to be *strong and courageous.* It was a command, not a suggestion, and God was saying three distinctive things.

### 1. Stand on His promises

The Joshua Project is based on this verse, 'leading people to inherit the land.'

Be strong (vs.6) because you will lead these people into what I have said is already theirs. This is important, as we are called to lead people to something that someone else has promised them. If Joshua knows that the Lord has already given the land to them, then that should make the job a whole lot easier. If God has gone before them, then

He will have prepared the way, so all Joshua has to do is walk in and possess it.

Forty years previously, Joshua and Caleb had seen the land and given a full report of it. Joshua knew that it was everything God said it would be, since he had examined it and had seen it with his own eyes.

What about our land? What has God promised us? We need to have a full investigation of the things God has promised, so that we know where we are taking people, and so that we can have confidence that the things we say about God are true. That means we have to examine the Scriptures and see what they say. If we do not have confidence in what they say, then we will not deliver our message with assurance.

## Can all be saved?

While I was training for the Methodist Ministry in Queens University Belfast, we did most of our studying in the Methodist College or the Presbyterian College. One tutor was absent with prolonged illness and a young minister took his place for a period of time. One of my colleagues knew of him and took him to task one day concerning his view of salvation. I thought my friend gave him a really hard time but in speaking to him afterwards I understood why. The young minister was working in a pastoral situation and my friend asked him if he could tell his parishioners on the way out of the church that Jesus died for them. The discussion went back and forward but eventually our lecturer said that *he could not tell any of his people that Jesus died for them because he did not know if he did.* In his view Jesus died only for the 'elect', and who was he to decide who the 'elect' were? Now I reject that thinking totally. Jesus died for the whole world and whoever believes in him will not perish but have everlasting life. I believe that all men need to be saved, can be saved, can know themselves saved and can be saved to the uttermost!

**You need to know for yourself what you believe, examine the land and decide what God is saying**

What about the things of the Spirit? Can all be filled with the Spirit? Can all speak in other tongues? What about healing? Is it God's will for all to be healed? Will God provide for our needs today? We could go on and on. Now I know what I believe about these issues, but that will make no difference to you. You need to know for yourself what you believe, examine the land and decide what God is saying.

There is a wonderful group of people in Acts 17:11 called the Bereans. They are described as being more noble than the Thessalonians. When Paul wrote to the Thessalonians, he commended them in 1 Thessalonians 2:13 for their acceptance of his word as the word of God. But in Acts 17 we read that the Bereans examined the Scriptures daily to see if the words that Paul said were true. The Bereans were familiarizing themselves with the Word of God and understanding the promises of God. That would help them to be strong and courageous and to have confidence when the devil asks the question, "Did God really say ...?" They could reply, "Yes He did, I read it just today!"

Hebrews 6:16-19 tells us that it is impossible for God to lie. He is truth in His character and in everything He says. There are many promises in Scripture that are given for us to believe and hold on to. In 2 Corinthians 1:20 we read about the promises of God. 'For no matter how many promises God has made, they are "Yes" in Christ. And so through him the "Amen" is spoken by us to the glory of God.'

This means that we can have confidence in the promises of God. If you are praying for someone who desperately wants to find Christ, then you know that the Scripture says that everyone who is thirsty can come and they will never thirst again. You know that in John 7:38 the promise is that streams of living water will flow from within him. Therefore you can pray with confidence with that person and say "Amen". God has guaranteed a promised possession. His Promises are true and victory is assured.

Look at a few of the places in the Scriptures where we are promised that we have the victory:

- Luke 10:19 – we have authority to defeat the enemy.

- Romans 8:37 – we are more than conquerors
- 1 Jn.5:4-5 – our faith has overcome the world
- Colossians 2:15 – the triumph of the cross. Jesus disarmed the enemy.
- 1 John 4:4 – greater is He that isin you than he that is in the world.
- 1 John 3:8 – The Son of God appeared to destroy the devil's work.

Joshua 1:6 "Be strong and courageous, because you will lead these people to inherit the land I swore to their forefathers to give them".

We will look at more of the promises of God in the chapters that follow. We need to know them and know what God has said about people so that we can have confidence in how we speak and pray. Then we will be strong and courageous just as God encouraged Joshua to be.

## 2. Stand on His Word

Verses 7 and 8 tell us again to be strong and courageous, only this time it says 'very courageous'. God tells Joshua to 'be careful to obey all the law my servant Moses gave you; do not turn from it to the right or to the left, that you may be successful wherever you go.'

In verse 6, God is emphasizing the promises and that He has already given the land to them. Here, He is telling Joshua to make sure that he keeps God's Word and commands in his mind and heart at all times. In fact he will need to be very courageous to do this.

Sometimes we will be challenged to stand up for what is right. When we lived in Wales, we did most of our shopping in Asda in Llandudno. I was there one afternoon and going to the checkouts I noticed the magazines alongside the tills. This is a common practice for supermarkets. You never plan to buy anything there but they want to tempt you while you are in the queue. Well this particular day they had a new magazine aimed at young women and the main story was promoted on the front cover, debating how crucial the size of a man's anatomy was. I picked it up and out of disgust went to the checkouts manager and complained. I was not really impressed with her reply as she was totally unaware that it was there and seemed disinterested, but I left my name and number and asked her to talk with the store manager.

So when I got home I wrote to the Asda HQ and informed them that I thought it was disgraceful that Asda was promoting such discussions about sex in a location where young children could easily read the cover. Very soon afterwards I had a phone call from the store manager informing me that he had removed the magazine and it would never be seen again on the checkouts of Asda. I had already sent the letter to HQ, so I sent another one saying what a wonderful man the manager was in responding so efficiently. We live in a market economy and your opinion counts. Stand up for what is right. Write letters to your MPs, state the case for the Word of God in our society.

Some of our laws, much of what we see on TV is against what we believe as Christians and yet, so often, we remain silent. Can you imagine some of the other religions represented in Britain keeping quiet in similar circumstances?

## The discipline of dedicated lives

Do not turn from God's Word to the right or to the left. Know what you believe and stand for it. We need the discipline of dedicated lives based on the Word of God. It is so easy to make little compromises along the way. I do not want necessarily to go back to the days when a Christian would never go into a shop on a Sunday and have all the shoes polished on a Saturday night and never be seen near a cinema. But the lines of demarcation have been blurred in recent days. Many Christians in Britain today are no different from their non-Christian friends. They go to the same clubs and laugh at the same jokes and the justification for it is to come alongside people to influence them with the gospel. It is a dangerous game when you consider that God said to come out and be separate and He set apart a people for Himself who were so different from the rest of the world. Compromise will creep up unawares and before we know it, we are far away from the place God called us to.

## No compromise

Look at Psalm 1. It is simply a Psalm about compromise. It starts off from a negative viewpoint. Blessed is the man who does not walk, sit, stand. There is gradual compromise here. He starts off walking with the counsel of the wicked. That is just listening to bad advice, not cutting it off at the bud. "I can watch this film, it won't do me any harm." "I'll go with them, I know they will probably all get drunk, but it's better that I am with them." Then this man stands in the way of sinners. Now he has gone a step further. He agreed to walk; now it is easier to stand with them. It was just listening to their counsel, now they are in sin. Then this man sits in the seat of mockers. It is easier to sit after you have walked along and stood with them. No Christian would ever set out to mock God, but backsliding is very rarely a planned thing. It happens often in church. A person misses a meeting, "Hey, it's only one meeting!" – but then they miss another, and soon it does not even bother them if they go to church at all. Compromise creeps up on you. We need discipline back in the church. We have boasted for so long that we are a people who have been set free from tradition that we slide away from the standards God set for us.

**Backsliding is very rarely a planned thing**

We live in a nation that leads the way in teenage pregnancies, under-age drinking, abortion on demand. We pray for God to bless us, yet how can He? I believe God is going to raise a new generation of people who will stand up for the truth, will be criticized for it, but will not care. They will be a radical group of John the Baptists who will prepare the way for the return of Jesus.

## The blessed man

Psalm 1 goes on to say that this blessed man does delight in the law of the LORD, and on his law he meditates day and night. Then he will prosper.

Another example of this compromise spirit can be found in the character of Lot. Lot lived a life of compromise. Because Abram and Lot's herds grew so much their herdsmen quarreled and Abram asked Lot to go in a different direction. Genesis 13:11 says that Lot 'chose for himself', and in verse 12 he pitched his tents near Sodom. Now even in those days Sodom was a name that equated to wickedness. An evil people lived there and Lot would have known that. But he still chose to go near it. After all, what harm could it do?

The next time we read of him is in Genesis 14:12. Some kings and their armies attacked the city of Sodom and carried off Lot as well as the others – verse 12 tells us that Lot was living in Sodom. How did he get there?

The last we heard he was just near the city. Well, this is the probable scenario; Lot was just outside the city walls and at night wild animals roamed and he got to know the people as they went in and out each day so they invited him inside. After all, it made sense, he had gone this far, why not move in, he would be safer.

## What happened to Lot?

We read of him one more time in Genesis 19:1. This time he is sitting in the gateway of the city when the angels, whom God had sent to destroy the city, came along. How did he get to sit in the gateway? Who sat in the gateway? In those days the leaders and Elders of the city did their talking and transactions at the gateway of the city. It was the place of power. Whoever controlled the gates owned the city.

What happened to Lot? Has God blessed him so much that he is now one of the important people in Sodom? No, he would never have been in the city had he not pitched his tents near and he would never have had a position of leadership if he had not moved in. The problem was that he compromised little by little and he fitted in so much that they could see no difference between him and them. But note this, **ultimately he had no influence** on the city, it was all destroyed anyway.

God said to Joshua to be strong and very courageous. Do not turn from the book of the law to the right or to the left.

Then God tells Joshua, "Do not let this Book of the Law depart from your mouth; meditate on it day and night, so that you may be careful to do everything written in it. Then you will be prosperous and successful."

The KJV says that you will make your way prosperous. In other words prosperity and success do not come by winning the national lottery or some vast amount of money, prosperity comes from following the word of God.

We need God's word every day of our life. We need to meditate on it and keep speaking it. Romans 10:17 tells us that faith comes through hearing, verse 10 says that it is with your heart that you believe and are justified, and it is with your mouth that you confess and are saved. Matthew 12:34 says that out of the overflow of the heart the mouth speaks. David says in Psalm 119:148 that his eyes stay open through the watches of the night, that he may meditate on God's promises.

## Meditate on the Word of God

We need to know the Word of God and meditate on it so that it will drop from our head into our heart, and then our mouth will speak what is in our heart. I believe that is the way God designed His word to work. He sent it and Isaiah 55 says that it will always accomplish the job it was sent for. God gives the analogy of the rain and snow coming down to water the earth. Their effect is to provide seed and food and so it is with the Word of God, it provides seed and food for us. Then we will go out with joy and be led forth in peace.

There are no shortcuts to this. It takes time to read the Word of God and it takes discipline to meditate on it. The picture of 'meditation' is taken from a cow chewing the cud. The cow chews the grass, swallows it into one of its stomachs and later on brings it back up again, chews a bit more and gets some more goodness from it. So we read the Word of God and later on in the day, think it over again and eventually we take in all it has to offer us on that particular day.

## Faith comes by hearing

Faith comes by hearing and that applies especially to the Word of God, but not to that alone. Whatever we meditate on will have an effect on us. Just think of the thousands of people who live for their favourite soap opera. I was preaching in a church one time and went to visit a friend of the Pastor. This man was telling us about his mother-in-law who watched all the soaps. Any that were shown on a different channel she recorded and then caught up on them every night. She watched hours and hours of them every day. This guy said he got into great trouble with her any time he suggested it was not the best use of time. Hey! Do not argue with your mother-in-law!

People read newspapers and magazines and without realizing it drink it all in. What you watch and hear will have an input into your life. Garbage in, garbage out! If we are taking in more of that stuff than we are the Word of God, then do not be surprised if you find it hard to believe God and live by faith, because there is more of God in a peanut than there is in the average soap opera.

Be careful choosing the films you watch. I was asked once whilst at a Ministerial Training College if I wanted to join a group of students who were going to watch movies all night. One of the ones they had chosen was 'The Exorcist'. Thankfully, when I refused, the guy said that he thought I would. I remember reading once about the man who wrote 'The Silence of the lambs' and it sounded very much to me like the man was in serious need of at least psychiatric counseling if not more. Again I was amazed at Christians watching it. I could go on and on here but enough is enough. If you watch every film and are not careful what you allow into your mind then you are an idiot!

God told Joshua to meditate on His Word. That means repetition. The messages that have blessed me most are ones I listen to again and again. Then eventually the penny drops and it registers in your heart. Then it really is yours and you can speak it. When I first visited Cathy's church in Newton Aycliffe before we were married, it was my first real experience of Pentecostalism. I was from the Methodist church and was very nervous going. One of the things that I found strangest was the number of times they sang the choruses or songs. I was used to singing hymns once through and then sitting down. Even when we sang choruses we only sang them twice through and even that felt radical. But they sang them again and again and again. They seemed to go on forever. One good thing was that if you did not know the song before you started, you certainly

**If you watch every film and are not careful what you allow into your mind then you are an idiot!**

knew it by the time you finished. However, after my initial questioning, I began to realize that many of the songs were Scripture, and as we sang them again and again we began to believe them, so we were singing proclamations of faith and they actually had an effect inside. I felt different when I came away from Cathy's church; I felt like something new had been established inside, and I believe the reason for that was the positive, Biblical singing that ministered to me deep inside.

So Joshua was to meditate day and night and God promised that his way would be successful.

## Prosperity

Just a note here on prosperity. It is a beautiful Bible word that has been misused over the years. There is no doubt that, according to these scriptures, the Lord wants to prosper us. What is prosperity? Is it having a big salary or driving a flashy car? I believe that it is having more than we need at any particular time. I remember going to Ghana several years ago which took all I had financially simply to get there. The children in the orphanage needed money and I did not have any. I remember getting before the Lord and saying that I would never come back again with nothing to give. Thank God that He honoured that. God prospers us so that we can bless others. I worry when people go on about what they have or do not have and I wish I could get them all to visit a poorer country and see some real needs. God took me on a learning experience several years ago when we lived in North Wales. We had been speaking at a church in the south of England and I had invited a family to come and do the Joshua Project with us in our home. They could not pay, so I invited them anyway and the whole family came. Now, as it happens, we had very little money. The church had given me a cheque for my preaching but I had no cash at all, coming home to a house with no food in it. When I arrived, there was a cheque for £1000 lying on the floor. I do not know how long it had been there. It came in the post from someone in Saudi Arabia. Now my question is this. When was I prosperous? Was it a few days later when I cashed it, or when it cleared my bank, or when I started to spend it? Or should I go backwards, was it when I told the family to come to our house? But the cheque had to have been sent before that. Was it when I prayed weeks before?

## Feeling and being are not the same thing

Now I felt prosperous when I had the cheque in my hand, but five minutes before that God knew that I would have it. In fact years before God knew that I would have it. You see, feeling prosperous and being prosperous are not necessarily the same thing. I believe that when our lives are based on Matthew 6:33 and we seek first the Kingdom of God, then He makes sure that we have all that we will ever need.

I discovered something recently about the word. Jesus was 'The Word' and I became intrigued by the verse where John the Baptist said that He (Jesus) must increase and John decrease. This can help us keep the Word foremost in our lives. Follow with me as I look at the voice and the word. The following verses show John the Baptist as the 'Voice' and Jesus as the 'Word'.

*John 1:21-23*
They (Priests & Levites) asked him, "Then who are you? Are you Elijah?" He said, "I am not." "Are you the Prophet?" He answered, "No." Finally they said, "Who are you? Give us an answer to take back to those who sent us. What do you say about yourself?" John replied in the words of Isaiah the prophet, "I am the voice of one calling in the desert, 'Make straight the way for the Lord.'"

*Luke 1:31&38*
You will be with child and give birth to a son, and you are to give him the name Jesus. "I am the Lord's servant," Mary answered. "May it be to me as you have said." Then the angel left her.

*John 1:1*
In the beginning was the Word, and the Word was with God, and the Word was God.

*John 3:26-30*
They came to John and said to him, "Rabbi, that man who was with you on the other side of the Jordan – the one you testified about – well, he is baptizing, and everyone is going to him." To this John replied, "A man can receive only what is given him from heaven. You yourselves can testify that I said, 'I am not the Christ but am sent ahead of him.'

The bride belongs to the bridegroom. The friend who attends the bridegroom waits and listens for him, and is full of joy when he hears the bridegroom's voice. That joy is mine, and it is now complete. He must become reater; I must become less. John the Baptist was the voice and Jesus was the Word. Therefore John 3:30 says, "The Word must become greater, the Voice must become less."

For the disciples this became a reality. They saw Jesus, the Word, perform amazing miracles and healings. They saw how, at his word, things happened. From the wedding at Cana ("Whatever he tells you to do, just do it", John2:5) to the Sea of Galilee ("We have fished all night, but because you say so, we will do it", Luke.5:5) to Peter about to walk on the water ("Jesus, you ask me to do it", Matthew14:28) to many of the larger group of disciples leaving Jesus and Peter saying to Jesus that they had nowhere else to go ("You have the words of eternal life", John 6:68).

**We are responsible for the voices we listen to**

Jesus walked in the knowledge that he had come to take over from the voice. There were voices everywhere. Voices can be good or bad, depending on the content. But we are responsible for the voices we listen to. In Mark 6:3, people took offence at Jesus and he could not do many miracles there. Jesus' response was to go around preaching and teaching the Word. We listen to voices all the time. That's why we change our car when we do, it's why we spend so much on Christmas presents for our children. It's why we feel we need to move house so often. Advertisers pay millions to put voices in our head. Teenagers sleep with someone to stop the voices. Kids turn to drugs and alcohol to satisfy the voices.

Here are four actions that will help us to earth this thought: How do we stop allowing the voices to rule our lives and tune in more to the Word?

**1. CLOSE THE DOOR!**

Jairus' Daughter in Mark 5:35-43

Many voices said that the girl was dead, but the Word said to not be afraid, just believe. How can that be possible when there is a dead body lying there? Well Jesus spoke the word and put the voices outside and shut himself and his 3 disciples inside with The Word. There are times when we need to close the door. Simply turn off every other voice and only hear the Word. Sometimes that may be people, sometimes the music we listen to or the programmes we watch. We need at times to take some physical action to put ourselves into the place where the voices of this world do not dominate in our lives. The Word must increase, the voices must decrease.

**2. CONTROL THE MIND!**

In the parable of the sower (Mark 4:18), the Word is choked by the thorns which are the worries of this life, the deceitfulness of wealth and the desires for other things. Matthew 6:33 tells us to seek God's kingdom first and then all other things will follow. To do this we need to take control of our thoughts. We need to take care not only what our ears hear, but what our eyes see. If we are constantly allowing our eyes to see what we know we cannot have, it will cause us to be frustrated and impatient and buy into the 'have now pay later' philosophy that is enslaving our nations. 2 Corinthians 10:5 tells us that we demolish arguments (voices?) and every pretension that sets itself up against the knowledge of God, and we take captive every thought to make it obedient to Christ.

Philippians 4:8 "Finally, brothers, whatever is true, whatever is noble, whatever is right, whatever is pure, whatever is lovely, whatever is admirable – if anything is excellent or praiseworthy – think about such things."

**3. NEVER GIVE UP!**

Bartimaeus had voices all around him rebuking him for daring to believe that The Word could change his situation. But he did not give up but shouted all the louder and Jesus came and spoke the word to him, "Receive your sight; your faith has healed you." (Luke 18:35-43)

Faith comes by hearing the message, and the message is heard through the Word of Christ (Romans 10:17).

**4. SPEAK THE WORD!**

Joshua 1:8 Do not let this Book of the Law depart from your mouth; meditate on it day and night, so that you may be careful to do everything written in it. Then you will be prosperous and successful.

Psalm 1:2 But his delight is in the law of the LORD, and on his law he meditates day and night.

Psalm 119:11 I have hidden your word in my heart that I might not sin against you.

Matthew 12:34 For out of the overflow of the heart the mouth speaks.

Colossians 3:16 Let the word of Christ dwell in you richly as you teach and admonish one another with all wisdom, and as you sing psalms, hymns and spiritual songs with gratitude in your hearts to God.

Romans 10:9&10 That if you confess with your mouth, "Jesus is Lord," and believe in your heart that God raised him from the dead, you will be saved. For it is with your heart that you believe and are justified, and it is with your mouth that you confess and are saved.

Ephesians 6:17 Take the helmet of salvation and the sword of the Spirit, which is the word of God.

And also speak it to each other…

Ephesians 5:18&19 Do not get drunk on wine, which leads to debauchery. Instead, be filled with the Spirit. Speak to one another with psalms, hymns and spiritual songs. Sing and make music in your heart to the Lord.

Jesus is the Word made flesh and he dwells among us. We can do whatever is in our hearts to do and we can be whatever He has called us to be but only if we allow the voices to decrease and His Word to increase.

## 3. Stand on His Presence

Back to Joshua 1 and verse 9. Be strong and courageous for I will be with you wherever you go. God is saying, "Stay in constant partnership with me." Continue with God even when things change. We must learn to listen and hear from God. That is the key to our strength. God is a God who communicates and desires that we walk in the revelation of His Word. How do we hear from God? Is it possible to know what He is saying to us? Is He actually wanting to speak individually to each one of us and guide us continually? I would answer an emphatic "Yes".

## How do we hear from God?

Let us look at 1 Corinthians 2. Paul is speaking about when he first visited Corinth. He had come from Athens where he had attempted to speak philosophically and argue with the great Greek thinkers. By the time he had arrived in Corinth he had given up that approach and realized that the wisdom of this world was inferior to the power and demonstration of the gospel, so he resolved simply to preach Christ. From verse 1 he explores the concept of hearing from God, how God cannot be heard in the normal way. In verse 9 he quotes Isaiah 64:4 "No eye has seen, no ear has heard, no mind has conceived what God has prepared for those who love him" – but God has revealed it to us by his Spirit. He goes on to say in verse 16 that we have the mind of Christ.

Now look at John 15:15 Jesus is speaking to his disciples; "I no longer call you servants, because a servant does not know his master's business. Instead, I have called you friends, for everything that I learned from my Father I have made known to you."

## See-Hear-Know

So God does want us to know His mind and walk in the revelation of His will for our lives. Here are some principles I have tried to apply in following the plan of God. I call it 'See-Hear-Know-the plan of God'. In Genesis 2:25-3:7 is the account of Adam and Eve in the garden. They were naked and felt no shame but they were soon to lose the glory of God. They knew God intimately, they heard Him speak to them. Adam was a spirit with a soul in a body. He communicated with God spirit to spirit as God is a Spirit. But when they sinned in the garden the Bible says that their eyes were opened, they heard the Lord God walking in the garden and they knew they were naked. Compare this with 1 Corinthians 2:9. They lost something in the garden and the spirit died. When we are born again our spirit is revived inside and God wants to communicate with us spirit to spirit.

## Leah and her children

Let me take you to an unusual passage in relation to this. Genesis 29:31-35 describes Leah, one of Jacob's wives.

Her desire was to be loved by her husband but she brings it to the Lord and has the battle and debate with him. She has four children at first and each one is significant in her quest to find God and the love of her husband.

a. **Reuben** means to see, and we need to see what it is God wants us to do. We have to have a vision. If we cannot see it then we cannot have it. Paul had a vision (Acts 26:17-20), Joseph had a dream (Genesis 37:5); without a dream, people perish. But a dream is not enough. Isaiah had a vision of the Lord in Isaiah 6 but it only filled him with fear until he heard the voice of the Lord.

b. **Simeon** means to hear, and after we have seen we need to have a word from the Lord. Matthew 4:4 says that man cannot live by bread alone but by every word (rhema) that comes out of the mouth of God. John 15:7 says that if we remain in Him and His words (rhema) remain in us, we can ask whatever we wish and it will be given to us.

God gave me Joshua 1:6 before I first started the Joshua Project. It was initially grounded in North Wales. People asked me to bring it to their church and then God gave me Joshua 1:9 and promised to be with me wherever I went. I was released to go around the churches. So in each major step I have taken, God has given a word for us as a family. But even that is not enough.

c. **Levi** means attached. In other words she became one with her husband. This is important. We need to become part of the word and the word part of us. That can only come, as we have been learning, by meditating on the word, living it, speaking it, dreaming it. The word needs to get deep into our spirits until it becomes part of us.

d. Then **Judah** means praise and when we get to that stage we know that the word has become established in our lives.

We need to See-Hear-Know the will of God, and it is possible. God will speak to you. Allow Him to give you a vision. Meditate on His word. Let it permeate your life. Looking in the Scriptures you will find examples of this process. Sometimes it all comes together. Take Paul for instance. In Acts 9, he sees the Lord, hears his voice, and knows his direction. In Luke 2 the Shepherds see the angel and the choir, they hear the voice, they go to Bethlehem and see and they return praising and glorifying God.

God has promised to be with Joshua and with us. Look at a few verses where we see the presence of God:

Psalm 34:7 – The angel of the LORD encamps around those who fear him, and he delivers them.

2 Kings 6:17 – Elisha's servant saw chariots of fire all around Elisha.

2 Timothy 4:17 Paul says that the Lord stood at his side.

## Therefore be strong and courageous

Joshua received the same instructions in 8:1 and 10:8. Then in 10:25 Joshua, himself, tells the people to be strong and courageous. Joshua has meditated on the word God had given him and now he is speaking it himself. This is the real proof that Joshua has learnt the lesson.

## Some further verses on fear

- 2 Timothy 1:7 – God has not given us a spirit of fear, but of love, power and a sound mind.
- 2 Timothy 2:1 – You then my son, be strong in the grace that is in Christ Jesus.
- 1 John 4:18 – There is no fear in love.
- Matthew 6:25ff. – Do not worry, God will look after you.
- Romans 8:39 Nothing can separate us from the love of God that is in Christ Jesus our Lord.

## Therefore fear not!

The command to "Fear not!" appears 366 times in the Bible, enough for one every day to even include a leap year! Look at a few of them:

Genesis 15:1 I am your shield.

2 Chronicles 20:15 – The battle is not yours.

Psalm 27:1 – The Lord is my Light and Salvation, the stronghold of my Life.

Isaiah 41:10 – God gives strength.

Isaiah 43:1 – I have redeemed you, I have called you by name ...

John 14:1  Jesus prepares a place for us.

## Chapter 5

# Crossing the Jordan

Joshua 3:1-5

*Early in the morning Joshua and all the Israelites set out from Shittim and went to the Jordan, where they camped before crossing over.*
*After three days the officers went throughout the camp, giving orders to the people: "When you see the ark of the covenant of the LORD your God, and the priests, who are Levites, carrying it, you are to move out from your positions and follow it.*
*Then you will know which way to go, since you have never been this way before. But keep a distance of about a thousand yards between you and the ark; do not go near it."*
*Joshua told the people, "Consecrate yourselves, for tomorrow the LORD will do amazing things among you."*

Chapter 2 brings good news, a good report; they can take the land.
*They will cross the Jordan river, when it is at its fullest* (vs.15); but not quite yet!

## 1. Camp before crossing over (vs.1)

I am a very active person and do not like waiting. I hate queues when driving anywhere and would rather go a longer way so long as I can keep moving. I feel that waiting is such a waste of time. Think of all the good things you could be doing whilst in the waiting period! The worst thing about waiting is when you have no idea how long the wait will be. At least if you know that the traffic jam is because of roadworks two miles ahead, you can see the wait coming to an end, or if you are in the dentist's waiting room and there are three people before you, then you can relax and read a magazine. However God does not seem to work like that. He does not give timetables for his dealings with us which is so frustrating.

What, after all, is the point of waiting. Why wait till tomorrow if you can do it today. But God says to wait. Camp for three days. They have waited forty years for this and still they must wait. The Psalmist puts it like this.

Psalm 37:7 Be still before the Lord and wait patiently for him.

Psalm 40:1 I waited patiently for the Lord and He heard my cry.

Can you imagine how the first disciples must have felt when they were told to wait? In Acts 1:4 we read that they were told not to leave Jerusalem but wait for the gift the Father promised. They were given no idea how long it would be. They just had to wait. This all comes down to a simple thing called trust. When we are in charge we can drive the agenda, but in matters of faith, God is in charge and He insists on being in charge so we just have to wait.

However there will come a time when the waiting is over.

## 2. Watch for the move of God (vs.3)

The Ark of the Covenant symbolised the presence of God; they were to keep their eyes on it. Similarly we must keep our spiritual eyes open and be aware of what the Lord is doing today. Communication has never been so good, and we can watch through the Christian media what the Lord is doing in different parts of the world with various ministries. The people of Israel did not know when the Ark was going to move, they just had to watch. The people knew nothing of God's plan to take Jericho and the Land. But God knew his own plan. God had a higher agenda and God will always work according to his own agenda.

Today we're seeing a tremendous move of the Holy Spirit. But we must never put him in a box. In John 16:8 we see the Holy Spirit's agenda, to convict the world of guilt in regard to sin, righteousness and judgement. Acts 1:8 tells us that we will receive power to be witnesses. John 16:13 tells us that He will lead us into all truth. God is equipping his children to do the work he has called us to do ... to take our localities for Him. We must move when he says so.

## 3. Leave your positions and follow (vs.3)

In other words, start to take a few risks, both as a church and as individuals. Deuteronomy 32:11 describes an eagle that stirs up its nest and hovers over its young, that spreads its wings to catch them and carries them on its pinions. So God will deal with His children. The way the eagle does this is very interesting. The little baby eaglet is enjoying everything in the nest, three square meals a day, tucked into bed at night, encouraged all the time. That can be a bit like the church really. However the time will come when that little eagle should be flying. There are heights where it was destined to soar and new things that it needs to see. But in the comfort of that nest it will never see them. Therefore mummy and daddy eagle, in their wisdom, start to pull away the feathers and the comfort of the nest until it starts to get uncomfortable and 'things are not like they used to be'. Eventually they will toss that eagle out of the nest altogether and the baby eagle will hurl towards the ground on its first bungee jump. Before it hits the ground mummy will fly under her precious baby, catch it, return it to the nest and start the process all over again. This is not an enjoyable experience! Eventually the young eagle will flap its wings and start to fly and soar as an eagle should, up to the heights that it was created for.

**God comforts the disturbed and disturbs the comfortable**

Then the eagle is grateful to its parents for being so hard and is flying by faith. For a long time the eagle squawked at being made uncomfortable in the nest, but now that it can fly there is no way it wants to go back. I remember being told at college that 'God comforts the disturbed and disturbs the comfortable'.

A number of years ago, I was invited to preach at a church in the Portsmouth area in the south of England. Cathy's grandparents were born there and as I was going down anyway, I suggested that they travelled with me to catch up on some of their family and friends. This was my first visit to Portsmouth itself, so I relied on them for directions. That was fine until we got to the city of Portsmouth and Nan decided to guide me from the back seat. It would have been very good if she had said things like, "turn left" or "turn right" or even "straight on at the lights", but she said things like, "go this way" or "turn there" and used her hands to indicate the actual direction. The trouble with that approach was that she was in the back and I could not see her hands, so eventually she would say, "You've gone the wrong way!" I was a nervous wreck by the time I got to their relative's house.

## "This is the way"

I have often thought of that incident when reading the following verse: Isaiah 30:21 'whether you turn to the right or to the left, your ears will hear a voice behind you, saying "this is the way, walk in it."' I would be much happier if it said, "There will be somebody sitting in the front seat alongside you indicating very clearly which way you must go!"

I think that the way God deals with Moses when He calls him is very funny. He gave him a great deal when He said that he would eventually know which way he should go because he would worship God on the mountain when it was over (Exodus 3:12). Brilliant! After it is finished he will know whether it is right to do it or not.

There are occasions when God leaves us to go ahead with what we think He has already said, and we just have to get on with it. There is a risk involved and a step of faith. But God is a God of faith and I believe that He always honours steps of faith, dare I say it, even when they are wrong!

We must expect God to do something different with us and be prepared for Him to launch us into something new.

In Verse 3, Joshua tells the people that when they see the Ark advance, they are to move after it. But he says to 'move out from your positions'. This could be really uncomfortable. It might have taken them a long time to feel comfortable in their particular place and now Joshua is telling them to relocate. We live in a world where people like to have a position and it can be the same in the church. It can be nice to have a title, a place that is recognised, guidelines and limits within which we function. These can be fine but when God wants to move us into the land of faith then everything must be negotiable. We may lose our respectability. Not everyone will want to live a life of faith and if you decide to do so, then you may throw a bad light on those who do not. However we were not called to be men-pleasers but God-pleasers.

## 4. You will know which way to go (vs.4)

Only then will we know which way to go. God only promises to guide us when we are already in motion. It is a fact that it is much easier to steer a car that is already moving. This is where the faith comes in. When we believe that God has called us and we have a word from the Lord, we then have to make a move. In fact God will wait until we move. Sometimes we want God to send us a personal letter and have it confirmed by at least half of the church congregation before we will do anything. But you are different. You are reading this because you really want to live and walk by faith. If that is the case, then do not expect God to give you the whole blueprint for your life before you do anything. You will be waiting a long time! God will speak to you and then sit back and watch you move. If you do not proceed then you will not hear anything else.

**It is much easier to steer a car that is already moving**

## I think I've been here before

Joshua says that they will know which way to go because they have never been that way before. Now when I first read this and thought about my Christian life, I had to ask myself some very searching questions. How much of my

Christian experience was just a re-run of what I had already done? Was I experiencing anything new? I have been at meetings all my life and many of them are repetitions of the last one. I have responded many times and gone to the altar at many churches and meeting halls and responded to the preacher's call but was anything different?

This came to a head for me one New Year's Eve in New Life Baptist Church, Northallerton. As was usual we met to ring in the New Year but at the turning of the year we prayed with each other at the front of the church and it was always a very moving moment. But on this particular year, I had difficulty remembering what year it was. It was a surreal moment, and I stood there remembering all the previous times I had stood on that exact spot and prayed the same prayers – and I wondered how many more years I would repeat the process yet again. There was nothing wrong with me or with the church and the people around me; I just felt that the years were piling up and the annual cycle was going on and on, but very little had or was likely to ever change. I was doing the same as the previous year. Allow me to ask you the same searching questions.

**Is our expectation of God based purely on what we have seen Him do before?**

Is our expectation of God based purely on what we have seen Him do before? When was the last time we did

anything different? Do we ever meet or make relationships with new people or do we always stay in our well-established circles? How long has it been since we visited a new place?
Joshua told the people that they had never been this way before. When we look through the Bible we see some in Scripture who went into places they had never been before and some burned their bridges so they could not return …

Elisha, in 1 Kings 19:19-21, after he had heard God's instructions through Elijah, slaughtered his oxen, gave it all away and went after the call of God.

Shadrach, Meshach & Abednego, in Daniel 3:16, abandoned themselves into the hands of God whether He saved them or not.

Paul, in Acts 21:10-14, was totally committed to the plan of God whether it meant blessing or prison or death.

The Holy Spirit is doing some new things among us, though many would say that they have experienced such things before. But God is doing a new thing, let's not think that we've been there before. God will lead those who are willing to be led along new avenues of experience and challenge that will influence their whole lives.

## 5. Keep a distance (vs.4)

Remember our God is a consuming fire and will share his glory with no-one else. Let us revere him. We live in a wonderful age of intimacy with God. Over the past decade there has been an upsurge of hymns and songs of worship which draw us close to the Father. Although inspiring, it can at times lead us into thinking that Jesus is our buddy causing us to become sloppy in our approach to God. Remember that God is the Creator of the universe. In the book of Job (from chapter 38), God reminds Job and his friends of just who He is and the things He has done, and how small man is. We live in marvellous days of grace and we trust in the shed blood of Jesus which covers us. Without that we could never appear in the presence of a holy God. One day this world will see the wrath of God but that wrath will pass over us, thank God!

### 6. Consecrate yourselves (vs.5)

Set yourself on the altar totally surrendered for God to use, or not use, as and when He likes. This is our response to God. This is our reasonable worship according to Romans 12. We are to offer our bodies as living sacrifices, holy and pleasing to God. The main difference between a dead sacrifice and a living one is that a living one can crawl off the altar and needs putting back there every now and again. Consecration means to set ourselves apart for God, to give Him all the controlling rights over our lives, our bodies, our relationships, our possessions, our plans. We make Him number one in our life and crown Him as Lord and Master.

Every New Year in the Methodist Church, the people called Methodists have what they call 'Covenant Sunday'. I have been to many of these over the years and they have been some of the most meaningful services in my life. Many other churches are following their lead in this, including our own in Northallerton. It is a service of consecration with the claims of Christ set out clearly and our expected response also set out clearly. As a church body we repeat the Covenant which reads as follows:

*I am no longer my own but yours.*
*Put me to what you will,*
*Rank me with whom you will;*
*Put me to doing, put me to suffering;*
*Let me be employed for you*
*Or laid aside for you,*
*Exalted for you or brought low for you;*

*Let me be full, let me be empty;*
*Let me have all things, let me have nothing;*
*I freely and wholeheartedly yield*
*All things to your pleasure and disposal.*

*And now, glorious and blessed God,*
*Father, Son and Holy Spirit,*
*You are mine and I am yours. So be it.*
*And the Covenant now made on earth,*
*Let it be ratified in Heaven.*
*Amen*

What incredible words! But I believe that we need to be reminding ourselves of the promises we made to God. God certainly does not forget them and we need to recognise that when we gave our lives to Christ we did just that. There was no negotiating going on at the cross, we simply surrendered.

## 7. Tomorrow God will do amazing things (vs.5)

This is the other side of it. We consecrate our lives and God will do the rest. He will perform the miracles He has planned that will surprise us – all we can do is to prepare ourselves. What a promise! God will respond to our sacrifice. "Amazing things" are what we do not normally see, exciting things, things that will turn the attention of people toward God.

# Chapter 6

# Circumcision at Gilgal

Read the whole of Joshua chapter 5 before you begin this chapter. The people have crossed the Jordan river, and are heading towards Jericho.

I am very excited as I begin to write this chapter. I think that it is perhaps the most important part of the book of Joshua as we see the basis laid for entering the land of faith. This is a very methodical, orderly, sequential chapter. It sets out the ground rules for our journey of faith. It realigns the thinking of the people of God and establishes them before they go any further. Now that they have come out of the land of Egypt it is time to get the land of Egypt out of them.

## 1. The enemy fears because of God's people

Verse 1 tells us that the surrounding kings were afraid when they heard what the Lord had done in drying up the Jordan.

Their hearts sank and they lost courage. How did they hear about all of this? Somebody, somewhere, must have told them.

There is a very interesting point here. We can compare this verse with Joshua 2:11 'When we heard of it, our hearts sank and everyone's courage failed because of you.' This was the testimony of Rahab in Jericho. Everyone was talking about how the Lord dried up the Red Sea and they were afraid. But in chapter 5 it is the Jordan. Here is a big difference, one which is very significant. Only Joshua and Caleb, of all the fighting men to come out of Egypt, survived to see the promised land. When Rahab recalled the Red Sea incident, only Joshua and Caleb were actual witnesses to it and so the rest could only echo what they were told around the campfires. It was history to them. They had no doubt that it was true, but nevertheless it was someone else's testimony, not theirs.

**This was not a mere bedtime story**

In chapter 5 everything changes. Every one of them crossed the River Jordan and every one of them saw the Lord hold back the water. They saw it with their own eyes; this was not a mere bedtime story. They saw it and they believed it and that is all there was to it. Why is this important? Well, we read lots of stories of how great men and women of old did great exploits for God. We read of Smith Wiggleworth and George Müller and we marvel at how great their faith was. We read story after story and hear from our pulpits illustration after illustration and, to be honest, I get fed up with it. We read these stories to encourage one another but often they are a long away from our experience. I have decided of late that I do not want to read another book or biography of the exploits of someone else; I want to see them myself. The world is fed up of the stories of how God provided for someone long ago or how God healed somebody in some other continent. They want to know how God turned up for you and how you were healed by the power of God. They want to see God working through you and not through some third-hand experience that may or may not be true.

Here in Joshua 5, all of the Israelites could give a personal testimony, "I was there. I saw the whole thing with my own eyes. I know it is true!" I pray that as you read these chapters a deeper hunger and desire than ever before will grip your heart and drive you to God to see his holy arm laid bare. These miracles are for today. The same power is available. God simply wants a channel to work through and you are that channel.

God had promised Moses in Ex. 23:27 that He would make all their enemies turn their backs and run. We are winners because we are on the Lord's side.
1 John 4:4 tells us that the one who is in us is greater than the one who is in the world.

## 2. The people are circumcised (vs.2)

(Verses 4-8 explain why!) All the children born during the desert journey had not been circumcised and so it was time they were. I drew attention in chapter 2 to one of the most frightening verses in the Bible. Numbers 14:28 says that God would do the very things that He heard the Israelites say. They had been complaining about the giants in the land and said that it would be better for them to die in the desert than to be killed trying to enter the promised land. God granted them their wish.

## Moving house

Whenever I read of that incident it reminds me of when we moved house to where we currently live. We moved from North Wales back up to North Yorkshire after God had released me with the verse in Joshua 1:9, where He promised Joshua that He would be with him wherever he went. As with all families when they decide to move house, we contacted some estate agents and had some details sent to us through the post. One house got my attention above all the others. It had everything I would want in a house and was much bigger but much more expensive than the others. I was due to speak in what is now our home church in Northallerton to take a group of people through the Joshua Project.

On one of the afternoons Cathy and I went to look at the house that had drawn my attention, and it was great, but in need of a lot of work and decoration. After one of my meetings a lady came up to me and said the following, "Kingsley, I don't know why I am saying this; our house is not on the market, I don't even know if we want to move, but I really feel that the Lord wants you to buy our house!"

Well I have to say that it was a very interesting conversation. We had prayed about our old house in Wales and God brought a lovely Christian couple along to buy it so we knew that the Lord was in control.

Well we had to go and view this house which was on exactly the same road as the house I wanted and had the details of. It was identical in every way, except that all the decoration was done and there was a wonderful sense of peace and tranquillity there. We wanted it – but it was even more expensive than the first one.

That is when God brought me to this passage of Scripture. I turned to Numbers 14:23 where God is fed up with His disbelieving children. He describes those who were unable to trust Him to lead them into the land of faith as treating Him with contempt. I stopped at that verse, wrote it down in my book and told the Lord that I would not treat Him with contempt by refusing to go for the house He had placed in our heart just because we thought we could not afford it. Well, the rest is history and we are in that house at the time of writing this book.

A whole generation of God's people wasted His time and their lives. What a tragedy! There can be nothing worse than missing the mark that God has set for us. Then we have another challenging verse, Joshua 5:7 – God raised up sons in their place. Can you imagine God replacing a complete generation with their sons just because they were too stubborn to obey Him?

## Temple Sowerby needs a bypass!

At the end of my time at Bible College in England, Cathy and I became engaged. I worked as a Circuit Evangelist in the Methodist Church in Ireland and travelled regularly across the Irish Sea from Larne to Stranraer and then on the roads across to Co. Durham where Cathy lived. I loved that journey and it was an exciting trip each time going over to see my fiancée.

I remember going along the A75, then down the M6 and across the A66 to Scotch Corner. The first town that you reach on the A66 is called Temple Sowerby, and when I first went through it there were banners and posters everywhere displaying the words, 'Temple Sowerby needs a bypass'. It struck a chord with me as I went through and I wondered why a town such as Temple Sowerby, which appeared to me to be in the back of beyond, would ever need such a bypass. I tried to imagine the background, as it is on the main route across the Pennines from the North West to the North East of England. All of the big trucks and especially the Irish lorries travelling through Scotch Corner came that way. I guess that these very heavy lorries were breaking up the roads and causing a nuisance to the residents. Especially with the Irish boats arriving at Stranraer or Cairnryan late each day, these lorries would be trundling through their town all through the night. Other towns had built bypasses so why shouldn't Temple Sowerby have one? Well, I felt God drop a thought into my heart.

Temple Sowerby is like a lot of us as Christians. When God wants to move and we feel the Holy Spirit bringing change into our lives, it feels like these articulated lorries. He starts to stir us and cause discomfort which we do not relish and sometimes we put up a banner or poster that says to God, "I don't like this, please give me a bypass!" That is exactly what those Israelites said to God. The scary thing is this: God will listen to what we say and give us that bypass and use someone else instead. God raised up a whole new generation to replace those who refused to obey and trust Him. We are no different. God is not bound to use us. God can choose to use whoever or whatever He pleases. If we refuse to obey Him, He will simply use someone else. But I do not want anyone else doing my job, what about you?

Verse 3 tells us that Joshua circumcised the Israelites. What did this mean? It was a command to Abraham in Genesis 17:9-11, a sign of his Covenant People. It also had spiritual significance, a circumcision of the heart. Compare the following verses: Jeremiah 4:4; Romans 2:29; Philippians 3:3; Colossians 2:11,12.

## The central theme

Circumcision has to do with the covenant. The central theme the whole Bible is the covenant. We have the books of the Old and New Testaments, the Old and New Covenants. In the Old Testament, every time the word covenant is used, the verb attached to it is 'to cut'. In our English versions of the Bible, the translators simplify the expression to 'making a covenant' but in the Hebrew, the expression is to 'cut a covenant'. Covenant making or cutting is a messy process that always involved the shedding of blood. Sometimes covenants were made between nations, sometimes between individuals.

In Genesis 8 and 9 God makes a covenant with Noah. Noah and all his family had come out of the ark and sacrificed burnt offerings to the Lord. The Lord smelled this and made some promises to Noah. Then on into chapter 9 He sets His rainbow in the sky as the sign of the covenant.

In Genesis 15 God makes a covenant with Abram. He asks Abram to arrange the sacrifice and God sends a blazing torch to pass between the pieces. God makes promises to Abram and shows him that his descendants would be slaves for a period of time, but that they would come back to their promised land.

In Genesis 17 God introduces the rite of circumcision as a sign of the covenant. Abraham and Sarah were given their covenant names and God promised that Abraham would be the father of many nations.

When the people of Israel eventually did end up as slaves in Egypt, they cried out to God to help them. We read this in Exodus 2:24, where it says that God heard their cries and remembered his covenant with Abraham, Isaac and Jacob. So why did God deliver his people? Was it because He felt sorry for them or because they prayed a lot? No!

He delivered them because He had made a covenant with them. Deuteronomy 7:9 says that God keeps his covenant. Psalm 89:28 says that God's covenant will never fail.

It is a powerful thing when we talk about the covenant. We have no equivalent in modern life. I guess that the closest would be the marriage ceremony. It is a commitment for life 'till death do us part' and is symbolized by the never-ending circle of the wedding ring. But in our modern society that counts for very little. It is easier to get out of a marriage contract than it is to get out of a hire purchase agreement, so it is very difficult for us to understand the concept of a covenant. I love watching football and in the past players signed contracts and stood by them, whereas today many of the top players swear allegiance to a particular club whilst, at the same time, their agent is negotiating terms with another club. We live in a society where money talks louder and carries more weight than honesty, integrity and trust.

**God delivered them because He had made a covenant with them**

## Cowboys and Indians

I remember being brought up on 'The Virginian' and the old westerns. Do you remember 'Medicine Bow' and 'Trampas'? If you do, then you are as old as I am. I loved the old westerns with all the horse chases and the good guys and bad guys. The films nearly always ended with the good guys on top. I remember the Cowboy and Indian stories and, in fact, spent hours as a young boy with my cousins running around their farm with a bow and arrow or a gun and reliving the films. I remember that, unfortunately, the Indians were often portrayed as the baddies and the cowboys as the goodies. But occasionally a relationship would be struck up between one of each and I remember that the Indian's way of binding a relationship with the white man was to cut their wrists and tie their arms together until their blood mingled and then they were pronounced as 'blood brothers'. This had the significance of making them real brothers and protectors of one another. It usually seemed to happen after one had saved the other one's life.

I believe that this is closer to the concept in Scripture where we see covenants cut between friends. David and Jonathan's relationship demonstrates this clearly. But before we go there, I want to explore further the Covenant that God made in the Old Testament and see how it developed with Jesus.

## Names

Names have always been a very important part of any society but never more so than in Bible days. My mother called me Kingsley because she simply liked the name. I do not, to my knowledge, have any relatives or ancestors with that name. It means 'the King's meadow' but I prefer to think of it as 'Kingsley, outstanding in his own field'. All throughout the Scriptures names had tremendous significance. People lived up to their name which described the character of the person and in many cases the name was changed. We see God changing Abram and Sarai's names to Abraham and Sarah. He changed Jacob's name which meant 'Supplanter' to 'Israel', the 'Struggler'. Jesus did the same in the New Testament. Simon was called Peter. Saul became Paul and so on.

## I AM

In the Old Testament, God revealed himself through his name. When He called Moses to go to Pharaoh for him and Moses asked who he would say sent him, he was to reply, 'I AM' sent you (Exodus 3:14). This was the Covenant Name of God, 'Yahweh'. As it developed a Jew would never use this name as it was much too holy. They took the consonants of that name and added to it the vowels of the name 'Adonai' developing the hybrid name 'Jehovah'. This name they could say. Throughout the Old Testament, at significant stages, God reveals a further characteristic of himself through this name.

For example in Genesis 22:14, we have the story of Abraham and Isaac on Mount Moriah. God tests Abraham's obedience by asking him to sacrifice his son, Isaac. Abraham is obedient, but just before he does it he is stopped by an angel of the Lord and God provides a ram to sacrifice instead. Then God repeats the wonderful promises to Abraham but reveals himself as 'Jehovah Jireh', the God who provides. In our English Bibles in verse 14 'LORD' will be in capitals to signify that it is the word, 'Jehovah'. So here we have a development of the revelation of the character of God. He has made a covenant with his people and part of that, from his side, is to provide for them.

When the children of Israel came out of Egypt and started to move through the desert, they came to a place called Marah, where the water was bitter. God told Moses to throw a piece of wood into the water and the water became sweet. God then promised His people that if they followed Him and kept His commands He would not bring on them any of the diseases of the Egyptians for 'He is the LORD who heals you'. This is 'Jehovah Rapha'.

## The character of God

We see a progression of the character of God right through the Old Testament or the Old Covenant, where we build up a picture of God. God's Name is very important. Here is a list of where we find the others. I have included the reference after the name and also some New Testament verses where we see similar things said about Jesus.

1. **TSIDKENU** = Righteous. (Jeremiah23:6,33:16) (1 Corinthians 1:30; 2 Corinthians 5:21)

2. **JIREH** = Provider. (Genesis 22:14) (Philippians 4:19; 2 Timothy 4:17)

3. **SHALOM** = Peace. (Judges 6:23,24) (Romans 5:1; Philippians 4:7)

4. **NISSI** = Banner. (Exodus 17:15-16) (Romans 8:37)

5. **RAPHA** = Healer. (Exodus 15:26) (Psalm 103:3; John 11:25)

6. **RAAH** = Shepherd. (Psalm 23:1; Ezekiel 34:15) (John 10:11)

7. **SHAMMAH** = 'is there' (Ezekiel 48:35) (Matthew 18:20)

The people learned what God was like through his name. He lived up to his name. He did the things that his name suggested. He was the God who provided for them, who healed and protected them. He was their shepherd and guided them and so on. But it gets much more exciting than that. Yes, God was all of this as a result of the covenants He made with his people. But then we move into the New Testament or the New Covenant.

## The Old Covenant

The Old Covenant was based on the blood of goats and lambs. They celebrated the passover annually and sacrificed a Lamb, covering their homes with its blood. Also once each year the High Priest would enter the Holy of Holies as a representative of the people and offer the sacrifice for the people so that they could be forgiven. On that Day of Atonement a goat would have the sins of the people laid on it, but this had to be repeated year after year. Right from the beginning God had a better plan. God had a crescendo orchestrated that would sort out the problem of sin once and for all. There was a man called Jesus, named as such because he would save people from their sin. He was born of a virgin, he was the Word made flesh. He was before all time and by him all things were made and in him all things were held together. John the Baptist gives us the first hint to his real identity in John 1:29, "Behold the Lamb of God, who takes away the sin of the world!" The disciples identified him as the one who could heal, who could provide, who would always be there. Indeed, he echoed what they already knew about God in the Old Testament. He amazed everyone in John 8:58 where he said that before Abraham was, "I AM". He made statements about himself, "I am the Truth, I am the Door, I am the Good Shepherd" etc. In John 14:9, Philip had asked Jesus to show them the Father and he replied that anyone who had seen him (Jesus) had already seen the Father. Wow! This was amazing stuff for the followers of Jesus. Some could not handle it.

## The New Covenant

Then it gets even better for us because Jesus went to the cross. He became the sacrificial lamb. He knew that he must die for mankind. Just before his death, he gathered with his disciples in the upper room for the Passover, what we call the Last Supper. This was something that every Jew was familiar with. They had a simple meal with lamb, unleavened bread and some bitter herbs and wine, but this time it was different. Jesus talked about it being the last time and that he would die. As he took the bread he referred to it as 'his body' and the same with the wine, 'his blood'. They all knew about the passover covenant that God made with them. They all remembered about the angel of death passing over their ancestors in Egypt and about the great deliverance that God gave them. But Jesus talked about the 'New Covenant' and they did not understand. Later on they would.

The writer to the Hebrews tells us a lot about the New Covenant. In chapter 9 he explains how in the Old Covenant the High Priest could enter the most holy place through the blood of goats and calves and then only once a year. Christ was the mediator of the New Covenant and opened the way to the Father through his own blood. Chapter 10 tells us that his sacrifice did not have to be repeated but that it was a once and for all event. Chapter 12 shows us how Jesus brought his blood into the presence of God and that blood speaks for us today. We see in Matthew 27:51 that the curtain of the Temple, which separated the most holy place, was torn in two from top to bottom. This signified that the way to God was no longer reserved for a few and for one day only, but that the way was open for all to enter into the presence of God.

## Jesus, the highest name

Paul, writing to the church at Philippi, gives us some further insight into it. He talks in chapter 2 about Jesus humbling himself and becoming obedient to death on a cross. Therefore God gives him the name which is above all names, that at the name of Jesus every tongue in heaven, on earth and under the earth will confess that Jesus Christ is Lord. This is fantastic because we have seen the importance of the name of God the Father in the Old

Testament; it was a gradual revelation. Jesus told his disciples that anyone who had seen him had seen the Father. He was the full revelation of the Godhead. Jesus fulfilled all these promises and attributes that we see ascribed to God in the Old Testament. Then he promised his disciples that they could do all that he did and could ask for anything 'in his name'. We see Peter, on the Day of Pentecost preaching in the name of Jesus. We see Peter and John walking by the Temple gate when a cripple asks them for money. Peter said they had none but what they did have they would give to him, "In the name of Jesus Christ of Nazareth, walk!" This is fantastic for Jesus promised them in John 14:12,13 that they would do what he had been doing, in fact even greater things because he was going to the Father, and he would do whatever they asked in his name.

**"In the name of Jesus Christ of Nazareth, walk!"**

We noted that God came to the help of His people in Exodus 2:24, not so much because of their cries, though He did hear their cries. The cries reminded Him of His covenant and so His response was because of His covenant. When God came to their aid just before they left Egypt, He told them all to sacrifice an animal and put the blood on the door lintels and posts and the angel would pass over when he saw the blood. In the New Covenant, Jesus shed his own blood. When we are born again, that blood is applied to our lives and we are washed clean. Isn't that wonderful? But not only that, we can enjoy all the benefits of the name of Jesus. He is our provider, our healer, our shepherd. It is not the amount of fasting and prayer, though that is good, that causes God to respond. It is the fact that God made a covenant with His Son, Jesus, on the cross that was sealed with his blood, and every time God sees the blood, He remembers his covenant.

## A scar for life

Let us go back for a moment to the story of David and Jonathan. In 1 Samuel 18:1 we read that Jonathan became one in spirit with David and loved him. Verse 3 shows them cutting a covenant. Verse 4 symbolizes this covenant in a very powerful way by exchange of clothing and weaponry. We will see later just how powerful this is when we consider that the New Covenant was established on the cross and some of the benefits of it are the weaponry and clothing that the Lord has given to each of us that love him.

How David and Jonathan cut their covenant we are not told. The writer perhaps assumes that everyone understands the concept so does not elaborate on the procedure. However one thing we do know; this covenant was cut and therefore will have been sealed in blood. It is very likely that both David and Jonathan cut their hands or more likely their wrists just like I observed in the western films and sealed their commitment to each other in blood. We are not told if they mingled their blood, but it would have left a mark, probably a scar for life as a constant reminder of the deep promises made.

What did this mean? Well they made such a deep commitment that each one became part of the other. If David got into trouble then Jonathan would come running, and vice versa. They became each other's responsibility. They would look out for each other, morally, physically, financially, spiritually. There was accountability between them.

**They would look out for each other, morally, physically, financially, spiritually**

In 1 Samuel 20:16, Jonathan and David cut another covenant but this time it goes further. The first covenant affected the two of them but this time it is made between 'the house of David' and 'the house of Jonathan'.

In this second situation, Jonathan was already defending his friend and promising to look after him, and the bond was stronger even than his bond with his father Saul. When they part company in verse 42, we get an insight into the promises made. The Lord would be the witness between them and their descendants forever.

Tragically for David, Jonathan and his father die on Mount Gilboa. We read of David's sadness in 2 Samuel 1. David is devastated and sings a lament for them. Verse 26 shows us how his love for Jonathan was deeper even than the love of a man for a woman and there is no hint of sexual deviance here. This is the depth of a covenant relationship.

## David and Mephibosheth

Then we have the amazing the story of David and Mephibosheth in chapter 9. It stands out in the book of Samuel as a wonderful description of the far-reaching implications of the covenant-cutting promises. David asks in verse 1 if there is anyone left of the household of Saul to whom he could show kindness 'for Jonathan's sake'.

This phrase appears twice in the story. The reason David is looking is because he made a covenant with the household of Jonathan, so it is for Jonathan's sake that he wants to show kindness. Maybe David simply noticed the scar which reminded him of the promises, we do not know.

So David finds Ziba who announces to him that there is still a son of Jonathan called Mephibosheth who is crippled in both feet. He is living in a place called 'Lo Debar'. Lo Debar means a place of no pasture. What significance that has for us.

Just imagine yourself as Mephibosheth. You are one of the only survivors of the household of Saul; you have grown up with the stories of how David was a wicked king who tried to steal the kingdom away from your father, Jonathan. After all, your grandad, Saul, would have told you many stories about his exploits and he was so jealous of David that they were bound to portray a negative picture of him. David is the one who has killed his tens of thousands. As far as you are concerned, David is a very ruthless man. He lives in a comfortable palace while you grovel in a place of no pasture.

## A dead dog

David has him brought from Lo Debar to Jerusalem, and we see a little into the thoughts of Mephibosheth when he comes into the presence of King David. In verse 6 he bows down before him and David proceeds to tell him what is in store for him **'for the sake of his father Jonathan'**. David promises to restore to him all that belonged to his father and he would always eat at the King's table. But Mephibosheth cannot understand why David would treat him like that, after all he is only 'a dead dog'. He has a very low opinion of his own status in life and is acting very much in conformity to the place where he is living. But David calls Ziba in and announces to him what he intends to do, and so the deal is done. Mephibosheth moves to Jerusalem and eats at David's table like one of the king's sons.

This story is full of parallels in the Gospel and has serious implications for each one that loves the Lord. The reason for all this kindness is not because David is a very kind king though that may well be the case. David's character is irrelevant here. The important issue is that a transaction was made a long time prior to this incident when David and Jonathan cut a covenant together in which they bound themselves not only to each other but to each other's descendants. Therefore the action on David's part was an outworking of this covenant. He had to follow through because of the serious nature of the promises that were made. Mephibosheth was a beneficiary by default. All he did was to be born into the family and that brought with it indisputable rights and privileges, of which he was completely unaware. Imagine spending so long in a place where there was nothing, while he had the right to enjoy all that the king's table had to offer.

**Mephibosheth was a beneficiary by default**

I hope you feel like jumping around the room right now when you begin to realize just what was accomplished for you on the cross. Just like Mephibosheth you may have been completely unaware of it. David and Jonathan made their covenant with blood and probably bore the marks of that forever. We do not have any marks on our body but the Lord Jesus Christ allowed men to take both his wrists and put nails through hands and feet, spear in his side. He bears all the marks of the covenant. This transaction was done without our knowledge. God turned His back on His Son when all the sin of the world was laid on his back. Jesus took all that was wrong with this world, the pain and the suffering, the injustices and sorrows, the sicknesses and sin and bore it all. All of history was torn apart and reordered at the moment he cried, "It is finished" (John 19:30). We are the beneficiaries of the New Covenant that Jesus established. Romans 5 tells us that we have peace with God through faith in Jesus and access into the presence of God. What a privilege! Ephesians 2:6 shows us that we are seated in heavenly places with Christ.

There are, of course, tremendous responsibilities that come along with this. Jesus chose his first disciples and us to go in his name. God is not willing that one human person would perish and therefore we have the task of telling people about Jesus. There are many who have never heard the Gospel. There are many who have no idea of what is legally theirs through the sacrificial death of Jesus. There are many who are living life in despair in a place called Lo Debar, and they have no idea that there is a king who desperately wants to invite them to eat at his table.

**There are many who have no idea of what is legally theirs through the sacrificial death of Jesus**

There are place settings all around the table waiting for the people to come. But many of them will never come of their own accord. Like Mephibosheth they are crippled in both feet. Circumstances have not been good to them. They have been hurt and abused. They do not know of the existence of such a table, but even if they did, they would feel that it was not for them – and how could they get there? Our job is to bring them to the table just as they are, still crippled and broken.

Can you see why it is so important that you discover your land? So many people are depending on you to possess your land. We need to taste of the table ourselves and know what we are inviting people to. Please, get up and out of your Lo Debar where there is no pasture and pull a chair in at the Lord's table. That is where the intimacy is, where you will laugh and cry, where you will feel the warmth, enjoy the good food, know the acceptance of the Father. It is fantastic!

Back to Joshua 5. The Israelites have been circumcised and remain where they are until they are healed. Now that this has been done and some of the legal ground established, they are ready for the rest of the chapter. As I stated at the beginning of this topic, Joshua 5 is very ordered. The enemy is afraid of them in verse 1, then they are circumcised – time to move on.

### 3. The past is completely behind them (vs 9)

The Lord rolled away the reproach of Egypt. Complete healing. Gilgal means to roll away. This is where God takes the Egypt out of the Israelites. Sure, they had left it forty years ago, but Egypt had never left them. They still grumbled and didn't believe that they would make it. They lived the same way as when they had their chains on. The only difference was that they were in a different place. They had not had a change of heart. We also need a change of heart to realize who we are in Christ. Otherwise we will live like everyone else in the world, controlled and dictated by external pressures such as our peers or the media. To live with under those pressures will kill faith in our lives. Faith comes by hearing the word (Romans 10:17).

We hear many examples of people who lived through the 'great depression' or the war years or the Irish potato famine. Those experiences can scar a person for life. They learned during that time to live with very little, to be careful not to waste anything, to turn off every lightbulb when not in use, to use just enough fuel to keep them from freezing, to always buy the cheapest product, etc., etc. But then when their circumstances got better, many still live dthe same way. Not that there is anything wrong with being frugal, I guess it is better than being wasteful. Nevertheless, we can live as paupers when the Father has made it possible for us to live like sons. For those people, they have come out of the bad circumstances but the bad circumstances have not come out of them.

**We can live as paupers when the Father has made it possible for us to live like sons**

2 Corinthians 5:17 tells us that in Christ we are a new creation, the old has gone, the new has come. All that hung over us from the past is gone, at least its power has been broken by the cross, and we can live in victory. Sometimes we need help to get to this position, and that is where good Christian relationships come in. We need each other to pray through issues that sometimes try to drag us back to what we have been delivered from.

## Enough is enough!

We need to be soft towards God and aggressive with the enemy. I watched a football match recently which was a violent affair. The players were arguing and pushing each other. The referee was having difficulty keeping control. The spectators, nearly 60,000 of them, were going mad, and all this for a crazy game of football. However I wish that we, as Christians, would get nearly as mad with the enemy of our souls. We are in a battle and we need to take back what the enemy has stolen from us. We need to get to the stage where we say to him, "Enough is enough!"

God spoke to Job (Job 38:11) and asked him if he was around when God made the earth or when He spoke to the waves and said, 'This far you may come and no farther; here is where your proud waves halt'? God was showing Job that it is God who is overall, supremely in control. When He says to something, "Enough is enough!" then it had better stop.

## Paul and Silas

Paul and Silas had enough in Acts 16:16-18. They were on their way to the place of prayer and this girl kept shouting at them. Now it seems that it only bothered Paul after a few days. He got to the place where enough was enough and confronted the spirit in her. "In the name of Jesus Christ I command you to come out of her!" At that moment the spirit left her.

Jesus had enough in Matthew 21:12&13. Jesus entered the temple and overturned the tables of the moneychangers and the benches of those selling doves. "It is written," he said to them, "My house will be called a house of prayer, but you are making it a den of robbers."

I met a lady once in a meeting who came up to me for prayer. She told me of her son who was taking drugs, had been caught in possession and so was in trouble with the police. People had advised her of various options but I said to her that her son belonged to God because of the covenant that she had with God. Enough was enough! So we prayed and took authority over the situation and claimed the promises of God for her and her son. When I met her the next year, the Lord had turned the whole thing around. The young man was no longer in trouble with the police. Instead he was doing well in college and phoned his mum before sitting his exams to ask her to pray with him.

**Who we are determines the way we act and speak**

We have amazing authority as believers and we need to use our authority. Who we are determines the way we act and speak. Paul said that when he became a man he put childish ways behind him! Psalm 8:6 says that God made man ruler over the works of His hands; God put everything under his feet. But further to that in Psalm 115:16 we read that the highest heavens belong to the LORD, but the earth he has given to man.

God rolled away the reproach of Egypt. It would never have power over their lives again.

### 4. They celebrated the Passover. (vs 10)

What a wonderful picture of deliverance from the enemy. They were to repeat it every year. Here we have a foretaste of Calvary! 'This do in remembrance of me'. The sign of the covenant was done, the reproach was rolled away and to establish this in their minds they celebrated the Passover. Sometimes, as Christians and New Testament people, we simply think of the Last Supper as the bread and the wine. Of course Jesus is the Lamb of God and so he gave new significance to the whole thing.

## Intricate detail

However, there was a lot more intricate detail to the Passover. There were all the bitter herbs and the fragrances, there were the questions asked by the youngest boy and the answers which retold the tremendous, miraculous story. There was the unleavened bread to show the haste and the cups. Now the cups were really interesting. I used to get confused when reading Luke 22. In verse 17, Jesus takes the cup and then the bread. But in verse 20, after supper he took the cup. In my upbringing I had only thought of the one occasion when Jesus took the cup. It reminded me of his blood which was shed for me and I always found it a very moving service. I guess I realized that it was a looking back to what had been accomplished on the cross as well as a looking forward to the day when Jesus said he would drink it again in the Kingdom of Heaven.

I especially enjoyed it in the Methodist church where I grew up, as there was a biblical build up to it and then we had to actually move to the front of the church and kneel to receive. I always found that a wonderfully symbolic act of obedience and surrender.

However I discovered, when researching the Passover for my classes in school, that there was tremendous symbolism in the cups and there are four that I want to mention.

## Four cups

In Exodus 6:6-8, there are four promises from God that are thought about with each of the cups taken at the celebration of the Passover.

The first is in verse 6; "I will bring you out from under the yoke of the Egyptians." This was the cup of salvation. In drinking this, the Israelites would remember how God had saved them and come to their aid.

The second is also in verse 6; "I will redeem you with an outstretched arm." This was the cup of deliverance. When they ate the bitter herbs it reminded them of how bad life really was there in Egypt. They were slaves and were treated shamefully, but the Lord delivered them. Not only were they saved, but they were taken out from under the power of the Egyptians who could no longer control them.

The third is in verse 7; "I will take you as my own people and I will be your God." This is the cup of blessing. They now belong to the Lord. They are his people and are blessed.

The fourth is in verse 8; "I will bring you to the land I swore to give you." This is the cup of anticipation. God's people were a pilgrim people and, as such, looking for a new country. What they now saw was not the end. They were to live in the anticipation of a new city, a new land.

## 5. They ate the produce of the land (vs 11)

For the first time they ate something that came from the land of faith. The Scripture says it was on the day after they celebrated the Passover, that very day, very specific. It follows, therefore, that it is necessary for us to have a true perspective on the cross and the complete redemptive work of Christ and understand the concept of the Covenant if we are to truly enjoy the land of faith. The Bible says that the just shall live by faith (Romans 1:17) and that without faith it is impossible to please God (Hebrews 11:6). God wants us to live by faith, though that does not necessarily mean living without a salary. Living by faith is simply living according to what God has told us to do. Then take note of the last point in this chapter.

## 6. The manna stopped (vs 12)

The very next day in this sequential chapter is when the manna stopped. No more manna, the moment they'd all been waiting for! The children of Israel were sick of manna, their constant food for forty years. But hold on ... the crops are not falling from the sky. Is this not all too much hard work? Manna provision required very little work, just lift and eat!

The fruit of Canaan, however, required working the ground, sweat, frustrations etc. However, the discipline of collecting manna served them well in the greater miracles that would face them in the land of faith. Many today want only manna-miracles, i.e. God, You do it! But God wants to work alongside us in the land of faith. Manna-miracles feed only one family and disappear overnight; harvest-miracles feed a multitude and multiply.

**Manna-miracles feed only one family and disappear overnight; Harvest-miracles feed a multitude and multiply**

Manna is where we can stay for too long. We attend church, we have a problem, we cry out to the Pastor, he helps us and then it repeats all over again. Manna is what we get in the wilderness. It is not brilliant but at least it is regular. However there is only enough for yourself and your family. Manna-eating is basically a selfish Christian existence. Just look after yourself and you own family. Build an empire for it, a fence around it, polish it, but impact only a few. The land of faith is different. It is much harder work because you have to dig up the ground and plant seed and wait for a harvest. But when that harvest comes, it will not only feed you and your family, it will feed those all around. Your seed will have grown into a plant and into a tree with branches, leaves and fruit, and people will come and enjoy its shelter. Not only that, but when your harvest comes, it will contain seed inside it for a further harvest, should you decide to plant it in good soil, and so your land and effect and ministry grows. It will not disappear overnight but will multiply until it affects nations.

Now, which one do you want to describe you? Where do you want to live? In the wilderness with manna or in the land of faith with good fruit?

## Chapter 7

# The Battle of Jericho

Please read the rest of Joshua chapter 5 from verse 13 and chapter 6 before you begin this chapter. The Israelites have crossed the Jordan, and are heading towards Jericho.

### 1. God appears to Joshua. (5:13,14)

I love this portion of the book of Joshua because it is full of surprises. Sometimes we think that we have the whole thing sorted and God does something completely different - He has the right to do things the way He wants to. Here, a man who describes himself as the Commander of the army of the Lord appears to Joshua.

Most commentators seem to agree here that this is an appearance of the Son of God before he came into this world as a baby. The reason for making that connection is because Joshua falls down and worships and the Commander seems content with that whereas an angel would not receive worship (Revelation 19:10). We need to remember that our Lord Jesus Christ as well as being the one who calms our fears is also the Commander and Warrior of Heaven. We are in a battle and although the outcome is settled and the work of the cross is finished, we have a lot of enforcing to do.

One of the most interesting points here is that he has a drawn sword in his hand. A sword is a very heavy weapon and is designed to sit in its holder until it is needed. I remember watching Mel Gibson in Braveheart using a sword which was heavy and only came out as the battle charge was being made. When Joshua meets this man the sword is ready and therefore we can conclude that the battle has already begun, or is just about to.

There are many verses in the Bible that talk about the sword of the Lord.

- Deuteronomy 32:41 says that the sword of the Lord shall devour flesh and take vengeance on His enemies.
- In 1 Chronicles 21:12 God gives King David a choice of punishment for his sin and one of the options is for the people to feel the sword of the Lord.
- Isaiah 34:5&6 describes the sword of the Lord filled with blood.
- In Revelation 19:15 we see a sword coming out of the rider of the white horse striking the nations.

In all these verses we can sense the wrath of God and the judgement side of His character. It is important to realise that God hates sin and the only reason that we are not and will not be consumed is because of the blood of Jesus. God cannot overlook sin; it had to be dealt with.

There proceeds a conversation between Joshua and this Commander. In verse 13 Joshua queries, "Whose side are you on, ours or theirs?" This was a very simple question and a simple answer was all Joshua wanted. However he did not get what he expected and was probably shocked by the reply. The Commander answered, "Neither, but I have come as Commander of the army of the Lord". What was he saying? Was he really implying that he was not on Joshua's side? Joshua wanted to be told that the Commander was on his side and that Joshua was going to win a famous victory.

**It is essential for us to realise who is in charge**

In Romans 8:31 we read that if God be for us, then no-one can be against us, so we know that in a very real sense God is on our side. What is happening here then with Joshua? I believe God is showing something very important to us. It is essential for us to realise who is in charge. God was showing Joshua that Joshua was not the one running the battle. He was proclaiming that Jesus, the Commander of the army of the Lord, is the boss and the main character and is in control.

As I travel around I encounter many different people and churches and ideas. We all think that we are right and God has given us the correct interpretation of what we believe. We have seen unusual things happen over the past few years in various parts of the world, peculiar manifestations as people have sought God in a new way. Some folk were praising the Lord for such signs; others said it might be the work of the enemy. I already mentioned about the people who tried to see if I was in a 'Reformed' box or an 'Arminian'. We have many interpretations about what may happen in the end times. When is the Millenium? When is the Rapture? Will there be one at all? Will it be Pre/Mid/Post etc.? When I am asked about such things, if I answer in a certain way then the person either warms to me or detests me depending on what they themselves believe.

**He was stating that the Battle was the Lord's and not Joshua's**

Here is the crux of what the Commander said to Joshua. "Joshua, It is not so important whose side I am on, but it is vital whose side you are on". In other words, he was not saying that he would not fight for Joshua, rather he was stating that the battle was the Lord's and not Joshua's. This can be a very liberating revelation. We get ourselves so frustrated defending God and putting Him into our little theological box that it can steal our peace and make us suspicious of everyone and anything that does not grunt in the same way that we do. Remember God is so much bigger than all of that and He is in control. If we have some of our thinking wrong about the end times, God will still do what He had decided to do anyway. I do not think that God will sit in heaven worrying that He has to change His plans because Kingsley has not got it right! When we realise the sovereignty of God and His overall control, then we can sleep at night knowing that everything is OK and we do not have to convert every other Christian to our way of thinking.

The motto of International Gospel Outreach, (see Appendix, page 185), is ‘recognising the whole church, reaching out to the whole world’. In recognising the whole church obviously we are talking about people who are born again into the Kingdom of God so there are some essential basic tenets of our faith. But in the non-essentials we need to relax and allow God to do His work in each of us.

In 2 Chronicles 20 we read of Jehoshaphat discovering that a large army was against him. He calls all the people together to pray, while he sets their cause before the Lord. There follows a very encouraging prophecy telling them that the battle is not theirs but the Lord’s. So Jehoshaphat praised the Lord and there was a tremendous victory.

Joshua realises that the Commander is in control and so he falls on his face in reverence.

### 2. He brings a message. (5:15)

Then Joshua asks his second question, “What message have you got for me?” Again, I think that Joshua is expecting a certain reply. He was wanting the Commander to say that everything will be great, that Joshua will win a fantastic victory and that God is pleased with him and so on. However again the Commander surprises him. His response is to ask Joshua to remove his shoes for the place where he is standing is holy.

I love this, especially as it is so far removed from my natural inclination as a fidget. God has been dealing me along these lines for years and am grateful. We need to stop and worship. Even though the Commander's sword is drawn and therefore the battle is about to commence, there is still time to worship. We were created for worship and it is the highest work and honour and duty. We must make time to worship. It is not just a prelude to hearing the sermon on a Sunday morning. Worship is the highest privilege the child of God has. Let us all take time to be in the presence of God just to recognise His value and worth.

**Worship is the highest privilege the child of God has**

Joshua was standing on holy ground because the Lord was there. We carry the presence of the Lord wherever we go and so can worship whenever we wish. On a personal note, I really appreciate it when I am in the presence of a worship leader who can bring me into real worship. I know that we are all involved and have a part to play, but I feel so blessed when I am led sensitively into a place where I feel God in the midst. Whether it is with old songs and hymns or new ones matters little, but I long for the place where the heart is touched, the eyes moist and the King is exalted.

Chapter 5 then finishes with a short but so meaningful phrase, 'and Joshua did so'. Joshua has learned to be obedient and so there is no debating here, just a heart that says yes.

## 3. Jericho was tightly shut (6:1)

Jericho is shut up securely because of the children of God. Jericho is a type or example of the enemy and the battles we have in our Christian lives. It is interesting that the enemy has decided to shut up shop because of God's people. He has put restrictions on his people because of God's followers. None went out and none went in. They were trapped inside.

I was at a large Christian youth event a number of years ago and I was involved in praying with some young people who had responded to the preacher's challenge after one of the meetings. Two girls had waited behind but only one of them wanted to make some sort of commitment so I talked to her waiting friend. She was about 14 years old and saw me as a boring older person who had massive restrictions on his life. I asked her why she did not want to make the same response as her friend and as we talked she told me a bit about herself. She had dabbled a bit in the occult and had nightmares every night. In fact she was afraid to go to sleep. However she did not want to have the restrictions I had in my life because she wanted to be free to enjoy herself. I told her that I slept very well at night, but she refused to accept that actually I was the one enjoying freedom. I have often thought about her when reading this chapter in Joshua, because it is the enemy that is restricted in the city of Jericho and not God's people. Contrast this with John 10:9 which says that God's sheep will be able to go in and go out and find pasture.

It always amazes me when I see people who have various addictions but feel that they are free to do what they want. The enemy has done a good job in them, cleverly disguising their bondage as freedom.

### 4. God promises victory (6:2)

We have already looked at the victory God has given us. Here He says clearly to Joshua that the city is his. He will succeed because God has said so. We will also succeed because God has declared it.

### 5. God gave Joshua instructions (6:4,5)

God gave very specific instructions for Joshua to follow which seem to be crazy. Walk around the wall for six days, then seven times on the seventh, then shout. Wow! This was going to be amazing. Can you imagine what Joshua's people must have thought when Joshua came back from talking with the Lord and explained it to them? They must have thought he had gone nuts! This had never happened before! No one had ever won a battle in this manner. There was no book to look up and see this pattern.

We are in a privileged position as we can read the story and we know that it worked – but how difficult it must have been for Joshua!

## David in the valley

In 2 Samuel 5:17ff we read of David being attacked by the Philistine army. They gathered in the Valley of Rephaim for the battle. Verse 19 tells us that David inquired of the Lord for a battle plan. That was wise, as David had never been in quite this situation before so he needed help. God told David to simply go and fight and he would win the battle. Clear instructions and David followed them exactly. Then we read in verse 22 that again the Philistines gathered against David in the same valley.

So here we have the same army for David, the same enemy, the same battlefield. Everything seemed to be exactly the same, so surely David would simply go up to them and win the battle. However verse 23 says that David once more inquired of the Lord for the battle plan. This time the Lord tells him to go behind them and wait to hear the sound of marching in the mulberry trees, and then to attack, and the Lord promised the victory. David realised that the Lord was in control and though the situation might seem the same to him, he could not see everything that the Lord could see.

## How to heal a blind man!

Again we see this theme in the healing ministry of Jesus. On at least three occasions he healed blind men.

- In Mark 8:23 Jesus spat on the man's eyes.

- In Mark 10:52 Jesus merely spoke to the man.

- In John 9:6 Jesus spat on the ground and put the mud on the man's eyes.

If we had only had the first one we would probably have today the church of the 'Holy Spitters' and spitting would be part of the curriculum of most Bible Colleges. But Jesus did not repeat himself and stated why he did what he did in John 5:19 – he only did what he saw the Father doing. This is a big challenge to us today. Often we try to copy what others do in the hope that we will achieve the same results. It happens at an individual as well as at a church level. We run the same programmes as other churches in the hope that God will bestow on our church the same blessings He has on them. The problem with that is that we do not see all that the Lord sees. Each church is unique and may require a different approach. We need to seek God for ourselves and do what we do because God has told us and not because we see someone else doing it.

So God has given Joshua unique instructions and Joshua sets about following them. I find it amusing in verse 10 that Joshua adds a bit to what the Lord has said to tell the people of Israel. Joshua tells them to walk silently and not say a word until he tells them to shout. I think he probably was afraid of them going around muttering to each other, "This is a jolly stupid idea, Big Josh has lost it this time!" He perhaps is remembering all his generation who died in the desert because of their muttering against the Lord.

## 6. Blow the trumpets (6:4)

Numbers 10:9 tells us that the trumpet blast in a time of battle will bring our cause before the Lord and He will remember us and rescue us. It was a sign of victory.

Cathy and I lived in Lisburn in N.Ireland while I was at college in Belfast. On one particular morning we received a bill through the post and did not know how we would be able to pay it. So we prayed and left the house knowing that God would come through and sort it all out. We were rejoicing and believing.

On that morning I left Cathy to work, then drove on to College. We had a little Mini Metro car. It was brilliant but quite small. However as I neared Belfast I hit a hole with one of my front wheels which probably was not such a good idea. The problem was that I never seemed to come out of it again. One side of the car collapsed and I drove on at an angle for a few miles till I got to college. I am not, by any stretch of the imagination, a mechanic, but even I knew that this was not good! So here we were; standing on the promises of God to pay a bill we could not pay and then bang! Another bill! I was not really pleased to say the least, but I rang a friend and sorted some things out.

When I got back home I heard a Bible verse whispered into my ear. This was the only time it happened but I actually heard it and so looked up the chapter and it was 2 Chronicles 13, the story of Abijah, a story I did not know.

Abijah was a good king and was attacked by the wicked king Jeroboam. He was outnumbered two to one. Then Abijah shouted to Jeroboam about how he was standing on the promises of God and how Jeroboam had disobeyed God. Then in verse 13, while Abijah was speaking, Jeroboam sent an ambush around behind them and, when Abijah looked up, he was surrounded by the enemy. This was where we were; we were believing God for an answer to prayer and instead of getting the bill paid, we were presented with another one. Then we see what Abijah did.

**As they shouted God delivered them**

- They cried out to the Lord (verse14)
- The priests sounded the trumpets (verse 14)
- The men shouted (verse 15)

As they shouted God delivered them. This is all about the power of praise. We need to sound the trumpet, expect the victory of God and then shout the victory. I cannot remember how the Lord sorted out our bills but I know He did. However the important thing was that we discovered the power of praise in these situations and that there are times to raise the battle cry.

## 7. Shout for the Lord has given (6:5 & 16)

The Lord 'has given'. This is very strange. I often compare these verses with Mark 11:24 "Whatever you ask for in prayer, believe that you have received it and it will be yours." There is something unusual and vital in this. God told Joshua that the city was his and yet he still had to go and get it. He said that they had to shout, for the Lord had already given it to them. We see the same in the verse from Mark. Whatever you pray for, believe that you have received it (completed tense) and it will be yours (future tense). This really does not make sense. From a language point of view it does not add up. There is a gap between the past and the future and that is where the 'faith gap' comes in. The Bible says that faith is the substance of things hoped for and the evidence of things unseen (Hebrews 11:1). If we can see it, therefore, it is not faith. Indeed we do not need faith if we can already see what we are believing for. So if you are being challenged to do something by faith, then you will more than likely have to move out into the unknown with nothing to hold you except the Word that God has spoken to you.

**There is a gap between the past and the future and that is where the 'faith gap' comes in**

This is what Joshua had to do. He told the people not to say anything until the moment where they had to shout and then, if God did not move, they were all going to look really daft. If you want to see God move in your life, then you are going to have to be willing to take risks and therefore take the chance that people are going to think you are stupid. The faith walk is no place for big reputations.

## 8. Warning (6:17)

God gave very strict instructions here that the people of Israel were not to plunder anything for themselves. Everything was to be given to the Lord. This was a big test for them; this was the first time that opportunity was going to present itself and so they needed to be careful. We have to be careful that we remember the Lord in all that we do. All the glory needs to go to Him. God is not in the business of promoting a big name. The biggest name is already in His domain and it belongs to His son, the name above all names.

**The biggest name is already in His domain**

When we sin, we affect everyone else. In 6:18 the Lord says that anyone breaking these instructions will not only bring trouble on themselves but also to the whole nation. We see the results of this when Achan stole some of the booty and as a result caused thirty-six people to lose their lives (7:3-6). We do not sin in a vacuum; we affect many around us, so we must be careful.

So we have made it to Jericho. This is a picture of the battles we will have in the Christian life and, like Jericho, our enemies will fall, if we listen to the Lord and do whatever He says. You were born for a life of faith, and when you walk by faith, doing whatever He asks you to do, you will see God move in your life. So it is up to you; there is a choice to make, battles to fight, nations to be won. So, go on, possess your land!

# Chapter 8

# Possess the land

## 1. Where is your focus?

This is an important question as we continue to examine the land God has called each of us to. We use our eyes every day to focus on things near and far. We are unaware of it and it is completely automatic. I use an automatic focus camera that is a brilliant and useful tool. Some camera manufacturers have even developed an autofocus system that can tell where your eye is looking and where its focus is as you look through the lens. So as your eye moves about and focuses automatically, the camera does also. Now that is clever!

However, the interesting thing about focusing is that the subject we are looking at remains unchanged, it is our eyes that make all the necessary adjustments. That is why camera makers had to develop a similar system for their products. So the question of where we are focusing is a vital one.

Two people can be looking the same direction but seeing two different things. Whilst in prison in Philippi, Paul talks about shining like stars whereas many would have focused on the cold or the lack of food or the pain. David understands this and states in the Psalms:

Psalm 34:5 Those who look to him are radiant.
Psalm 121:1 I lift up my eyes to the hills.

We have many examples of focusing in Scripture:

(a) 2 Kings 6:16&17 Elisha was focused on something further than the enemy. He was focused on the presence of God. His servant had been focussing on the enemy and so it had changed him and led him to a position of fear. After Elisha prayed, his focus changed.

(b) Numbers 13:30&33 The ten spies were also led into a place of fear because their focus was on the size of the enemy. Caleb was focused on something greater than the size of the enemy. He was focused on the command God had given them. This changed him and led him into faith and peace.

(c) Hebrews 11:26 Moses was focused on something beyond the treasures of Egypt. He was focused on his eternal reward. Had he been focussing purely on Egypt and its treasures, it would have changed him and led to a different course of action. However he was able to choose as he did because of his long-range focus.

(d) Hebrews 12:2 Jesus was focused on something beyond the cross. He was focused on the joy set before him, and we are encouraged in the same verses to fix our focus on him. Then we will change and become more like him.

(e) Acts 7:55 Stephen was focused on something beyond the stones. He was focused on heaven and Jesus. I find this one amazing as those stones were so painful to him. However the Bible tells us that his face was like the face of an angel, he saw past the stones and changed, and God brought him home.

(f) 2 Corinthians 3:18 We, as we reflect, contemplate, behold and focus on the glory of the Lord, are being transformed from one degree of glory to another. We will change, and this has been God's plan all along. Before God ever wants to change our circumstances, He wants to change us.

(g) Genesis 13:14-18 The LORD said to Abram after Lot had parted from him, "Lift up your eyes from where you are and look north and south, east and west. All the land that you see I will give to you and your offspring forever. I will make your offspring like the dust of the earth, so that if anyone could count the dust, then your offspring could be counted. Go, walk through the length and breadth of the land, for I am giving it to you." So Abram moved his tents and went to live near the great trees of Mamre at Hebron, where he built an altar to the LORD.

Abram & Lot *saw* the same things but they were not *focused* on the same things. Lot saw what he liked and chose for himself. That is the spirit of the age, one of selfishness. Lot signifies the old way of living – looking after Number One. Abram signifies God's way, he was the chosen leader of God. There had to be a significant break from the old way of living. Verse 14: The Lord spoke to Abram ***after*** Lot had departed from him. God gives specific instructions: Verse 14 – "Lift up your eyes and look north and south, east and west; it all belongs to you." God had made massive promises to Abram and was getting him to refocus here. In verse 17 God says, "Go and walk through the length and breadth of it." Just as Joshua was told, put your feet on the ground. Then we see Abram's response:
Verse 18 Abram moved his tents and went and he built there an altar to the Lord.

Abram's focus caused him to make changes in his life. He had to move to where his eyes allowed him to see. The same will happen to us as we lift our eyes to see the incredible potential there is in God's plans for our lives.

## 2. Possess your possession

We need to understand just what the Lord has made available for us and it may help us to elaborate a little on Abraham. God made many promises to him and we have already mentioned them in relation to the Covenant. However the promises of Abraham are applicable to us today. In fact the Bible says that the Lord will keep His covenant to a thousand generations - we have not come a thousand generations from Abraham yet. (1 Chronicles 16:15&16)

Abraham, as a character, has been of particular blessing to me in my ministry and life. He receives many promises from God and then God gives him and Sarah the long awaited son, Isaac. They are so blessed as a family. But, in Genesis 22, God asks Abraham to give up his son. We cannot begin to imagine what that must have been like for Abraham. I do not know if he would have dared to discuss the issue with Sarah; otherwise I think she would have killed him! In reading through that amazing chapter I discovered a few key points.

**Isaac was not the answer or the fulfillment to Abraham's dream**

Isaac was not the answer or the fulfillment to Abraham's dream. The promise of God was that God would bless Abraham and make his descendants as numerous as the stars in the sky or the sand on the seashore. Isaac was simply the means to an end. He was the method that God would use to fulfill this dream.

Abraham set off with his servants, his son and the fire for the sacrifice but in verse 5 he instructed his servants to stop and await their return. God took Abraham as far as he could take him in a group. Now it was time for him to go it alone with nothing but his dream to keep him company. But then, in verse 7, his heart/dream/mind starts speaking to him and asking difficult questions. "Are you sure you heard from

God?" "Were we right to do this?" "Where is God now?" "You trusted in Him to provide, now look at you!" This is what Isaac was, in effect, saying. "I see the fire and the wood but where is the lamb for the sacrifice?" Then Abraham, the man of faith, pronounces, "God Himself will provide". Abraham continues and is about to sacrifice his son when the angel stops him and the rest is history.

We must first settle the fact, that, by faith, we are the children of Abraham. (Acts 3:25; Galatians 3 especially verse 14). God redeemed us in order that the blessing given to Abraham might come to the Gentiles through Christ Jesus, so that by faith we might receive the promise of the Spirit.

## Encouraging promises

God always promises to honour those who honour Him. And so in response to Abraham's faithful struggle, God encourages him with the following promises in verses 17 & 18. He says 4 things that are relevant for us today:

(a) Firstly, God promised to bless Abraham and He has promised to bless us. We are His special children, therefore we can expect our heavenly Father to bless us. So today, if you need to, please change your thinking to expect the blessing of God. Most people in the world wait for bad things to happen and we read/listen to/observe so many bad things. We therefore MUST lift our eyes to the hills and get our strength from the Lord.

(b) Secondly, God said to Abraham that He would multiply him. In other words he would reproduce the promise that was made to him. Whatever God has promised you, you will be a carrier of that promise. You will transmit that blessing wherever you go and people will start to be blessed simply because of you, for Jesus is in you. He is the hope of glory and the springs that have been building up in you over the years will flow out to others carrying blessing with them. What a promise! Today you will be a blessing to someone.

(c) Thirdly, God promised that Abraham's descendants would have victory over the enemy. Your family and those to whom God has called you to minister will be blessed themselves, and they will cause the enemy to flee from them. So your ministry will be effective in them. They will go on to know Christ themselves, not always needing to come running to you, but will have their own victories. Your life will have impact and results which will overflow to those who receive from you, so that they can increase in their ministry and life. You will be like a rolling snowball that gathers momentum and more snow as it goes along - your life will see increase, openly displayed through the lives of others.

(d) Fourthly, God promises Abraham that through his seed all nations will be blessed. This is the crux of this passage. Many Christians feel that God has called them to their locality, full-stop. I am not saying this because

I have a world vision. I am emphasizing this because of the promises to Abraham. Every single Christian ought to have a worldview. Every Christian ought to be aware of other countries. Why? Because God promised to Abraham and also to you, that you will cause all nations to be blessed. Some of you are preachers, some work from home, some of you in different nations, but ALL called to the nations. Not all will go but all need to be aware and gather the knowledge of what is going on. God called you to be a world changer. Don't allow the enemy to imprison you in your thinking. Cast aside a worldly view and get a worldview, see the fields as white unto harvest. You are far more than what you see at present. Get ready for increase, plan for it, make room for it, expect it and pray for it. Get alongside other world changers and talk it, read it, write it, become it and together we will become far more than what we appear to be right now.

**God called you to be a world changer**

Possess what God has possessed for you. That is the message of the book of Joshua. In the events following chapter 6 there are more lessons, but they concern mainly Joshua's instructions for the dividing of the land until we come to chapter 18.

### 3. How long will you wait?

How long will you wait before you begin to take possession of the land (18:3)? It seems that some of the tribes had no sense of urgency among them at all. So Joshua delivers a challenge to them. He tells them to get on with it! Look at chapter 17 and note the response of Manasseh and Ephraim. They were complaining in verses 14-18 that the land they had been given was too small. So Joshua told them to have the mountain country as well. Once more they said it was not enough, so Joshua told them to clear the trees and get on with it. We see then in Judges 1:27 that they did not even do that.

The same challenge comes to you today: How long will you wait before you begin to put into action what God has said to you? When God has challenged us to do something, I believe that He waits for a response before He will do anything else. Therefore the onus is on us to be obedient and to move ahead.

Look at Caleb in chapter 14:6-14. In verse 12 he asks Joshua to give him the mountain that was promised him by Moses. He was determined to possess his possessions and neither age, ability or circumstances would be allowed to stand in his way.

## 4. Survey (18:4) and Write (18:9)

Joshua asked the Israelites to send out men to survey the land. They were to examine the region and write down a description of each part of it and then return to Joshua. Joshua got them to write the descriptions down in a book. I have always recommended people to do this. I have done it myself on many occasions and still have the book that I have used for years and regularly go through it to see how the plan of God is working out.

We live in a generation that forgets so easily. We have many gadgets that do all our remembering for us and our minds become lazy. I find it extremely helpful to write things down. Perhaps you are reading the Bible when a verse 'jumps out'. If you feel that the Lord is saying something, then write it down. Perhaps someone shares a word with you which strikes a chord in your heart – write it down. Perhaps you hear on television or read in a book something that stirs you – write it down. Soon you will notice a pattern in your book that is helpful in analyzing what the Holy Spirit may be saying to you.

Also at major crisis times, when I have been seeking the Lord regarding a significant move, I have written my vision down on a piece of paper. I urge you to do this. Simply jot down what you feel the Lord has been saying to you, what gifts you have, what your desires and dreams are. Place it before the Lord and see what happens. This can be a very liberating experience, especially if we have allowed people and circumstances to force us into a mould where we find ourselves doing some things that we do not really feel that God has called us to do.

### 6. Bring it back to the Lord (18:6,9)

The men who surveyed the land were to come back with all their bits of paper to Joshua who was going to cast lots for them and divide it out. We need to bring our survey back to the Lord also. I think it can be helpful if we have some other Christian who knows us, and who we trust to share this with. Then together you can pray over it and gain the support you need. This will also give a level of accountability, in that the other person will probably keep asking you how you are getting on.

Then we need to bring it back to the Lord. We need to remind God of what He has said to us. This will cement the matter in our own heart, it will tell the enemy to watch out and it will thrill God that his word has taken root inside. Then when situations seem to be against us, we can take the word that God has spoken and use it against the enemy and circumstances and fight with it. This is what it means in Ephesians 6:17. Take the sword of the Spirit which is the word of God and use it.

This is what Caleb did when he reminded Joshua in chapter 14 of the word that had been given to him by Moses. He would not let go of it and obtained what he asked for. God loves that sort of assertiveness and says of Caleb that he had a different spirit. (Numbers 14:24)
We need to come before the Lord, write down our vision or dream, the details we have been thinking of, and bring it back to the Lord. As you begin to put this into practice it will amaze you to see how the Lord has been working it all out. It is enormously rewarding and encouraging and helps us to feel that we have been obedient to what He has called us to do.

# Chapter 9

# The effects of living in the land

In this chapter I want to take an overview of the Book of Joshua and ask the question, "What will be the effects of my living in the land of faith?" Some of these are by-products, I believe, of our obedience.

## 1. People will get saved

In Joshua chapter 2 we read of a lady called Rahab and her family. We get some insights into the enemy camp here and see what is going on. Joshua sent spies into the land. For a long time the Israelites believed that the enemy was terrifying, but actually, here we see that the enemy is afraid of the people of God.

- Verse 8 The enemy was afraid of the people of God - at least of those who would dare to possess the land!
- Verse 10 The enemy had heard of all the miracles that God had done.
- Verse 11 The enemy's courage failed.

Rahab was saved almost indirectly – it was not the main aim of the mission; possessing the land was. Yet, in possessing the land, people were won. I believe that when a person takes a step of faith, it will have an effect on their neighbourhood or circle of acquaintances. People will want to know Jesus as a result.

## 2. You will experience the God of miracles

Joshua 3:15 – As soon as their feet touched the water's edge, the water stopped flowing. God moved as their faith was put into action. Then they had to erect a memorial (4:5 & 4:20-24), as an everlasting memory to the God of miracles. As we move into the land of faith, we do our part in trusting God. This releases God to do His part and meet our faith with His faith. Then all things are possible. Just remember that, for a miracle to happen, you must have an impossible situation. If you can work it out all by yourself, then the Lord will allow you to.

**For a miracle to happen, you must have an impossible situation**

## 3. You will experience the awe of God

Joshua 5:13-15 – Joshua comes face to face with an angel. By possessing the land, they are moving more & more in a spiritual realm and so are open more to visitations from the Lord. We do not hear a lot of stories these days of encounters with angels, although we may have met many of them unawares. But, I believe that, as we move by faith, we are entering an environment where the supernatural and the natural converge, and we may at times catch a glimpse of what God sees.

### 4. You will experience victory over the enemy

Joshua 6 Joshua and his people have complete victory over Jericho and we are promised total victory in our lives. We are told in 1 Chronicles 20:15-17 that God fought for His people.

### 5. You will experience temptation

In Joshua 7, Joshua had given strict instructions not to touch any of the devoted things (6:18), but Achan did. You *will* experience temptation in the land, perhaps all the more. After all, there is little temptation in the desert. You are not likely to want to steal buckets of sand!

**You are not likely to want to steal buckets of sand!**

In the land that God has given you there is tremendous prosperity. With success comes temptation, and many fall into it. God promised Joshua prosperity (1:8) and success. We have to watch and pray lest we fall into temptation. This is where good friends can keep a watch over us and keep us on the straight and narrow.

There is a warning in Deuteronomy 8:1-14. Verse 11 cautions us to not forget the Lord our God, lest when we are blessed with material things, we allow pride to fill our hearts and we relegate God to the back seat in our life. Paul says in Philippians 4:11-13 that he has learned the secret of being content in every situation. It took him some time to learn it, but it was an important lesson and we need to take heed.

We will all be tempted as it says in 1 Corinthians 10:12-13. But we will not be tempted beyond what we can bear. Jesus was tempted (Hebrews 2:18 and 4:14-16); Achan did sin and brought destruction to Israel (6:18; 7:5). The sin was stamped out (7:26) and Achan was removed from the land.

### 6. You will experience challenge and renewal

Joshua 8:30. The people were called to make new commitments. As we move on with God, He will bring us further into the land of faith. I believe that there will be times when He shines the spotlight on areas of our hearts which we did not even realise were not surrendered to Him. It will be an ongoing process.

### 7. You will affect others by your faith

In Joshua 11:23 Joshua gave the land to others as an inheritance. He passed it on. We have the amazing story of Stephen in the book of Acts.

- In Acts 6:5 he is a deacon.
- In Acts 6:8 he is full of faith and did great wonders and signs among the people.
- In Acts 6:15 he has the face of an angel.
- In Acts 7:55 he saw heaven opened.
- In Acts 8:1 Saul was there giving approval to his death.

- In Acts 22:20 Later on Paul relates how this experience had a lasting effect on him.

The steps of faith that we take will affect other people. They will be encouraged to do the same. In fact, I believe that people are watching us right now to see what we will do. Conversely, if we do not take those steps, we may hinder others from launching out by faith.

## 8. You will experience the faithfulness of God

In Joshua 21:45 and 23:14, we read that not one of the good promises of God has failed. What a fantastic testimony! We need to listen to older Christians and this was Joshua speaking shortly before he was going to die. He could say this with confidence because he had lived a life of faith. We will be able to say the same if we launch into our land of faith.

So there we have it. What a blessing is waiting for us, and others, if we move!

## Chapter 10

# Conclusion ... or the Beginning

Well done. You have made it to the conclusion, or is it just the beginning? In this book, I have sought to stir your heart to see the impossible.

For Joshua it must have been an incredible experience to see the tribes possessing their lands. I guess it would have made all the pain worth while. We have examined him from his small beginnings as the trainee of Moses. We have watched him as he has been nurtured and shaped by God over a long period of time, long before he realised that the Lord had him marked out for leadership. We have watched his actions and reactions, observed his leadership qualities and seen the challenges put before him by God. He had to show himself strong and not fear, to rely fully on the word of God. He took amazing steps of faith, sometimes all on his own with the loneliness that faith can bring. He led his people well and kept his eyes on God. He tested the promises of God and found that they were totally reliable.

So what about you? What is your land of faith? Has God prompted you to make any changes to what you are doing? Is there a new excitement welling up within you, crying out for God to do something new in your life?

Well, let me encourage you. God only disturbs us when He is getting ready for the next phase. I am sure that the reason God prompted me to write this book was for you. God saw the dissatisfaction in your heart and wanted to bring you a bit higher. He is stretching you today and getting ready to launch you out into a new walk with Him.

I have found that any time I have been prompted to make a new step with God, something happens inside me. I change and get indelibly marked by God. I could never go back – where would I go? To walk with God is the most exciting life there is. Anything is possible. There are no limits, the horizons are extended and all things are possible. Get up and tell God that you are ready to go. Get out of that boat and start walking. If you are a young man, start seeing visions; if you are older, start dreaming dreams.

Get ready, put on your trainers, get on the starting blocks – you will never be the same again.

May God bless you as you walk with Him!

# Appendix I

This is a very simple exercise that should be both fun and informative. It is based on the principle that God usually starts where we are and uses what we do have before He expects us to believe for what we do not yet have. When He called Moses from among the sheep at the far side of the desert, he asked him a basic question, “What is in your hand?” The answer was an easy one for Moses because he was a shepherd. He, therefore, had a staff in his hand. God then instructs Moses to use that staff at some crucial times in his life. For example, when Moses led the people across the Red Sea, God asked Moses to stretch out his staff. When Joshua fought the Amalekites, Moses had the staff in his hands. So it continues through the book of Exodus.

Many Christians are very quick in telling God what they cannot do, when He already knows that. For example, I have had a number of people say to me that they are not ‘an up-front’ type of person, and that is fine. God does not want everyone to be a preacher or singer, but He does want us to do something, and He has gifted us all in some way.

The following exercise will help you to identify the sorts of gifts or talents that you feel God has given you. I would encourage you to major on them, develop them and forget about the rest for the time being.

On the next two pages is a list of 36 statements about you. Read each one and grade yourself from 0-5 for each. The first says, "I am handy at most things". Well, if you do not know one end of a hammer from the other then give yourself a 0 or 1 for that. But if you do get excited in prayer meetings, then give yourself a 4 or 5 for question number 2. Fill in the answers in the grid at the bottom in the appropriate box, corresponding to the number of the question.

Then you will see twelve boxes with a letter in each. Add up the numbers in the three boxes to the left of each letter and put the total in the lettered box. You will end up with twelve totals. Then take a note of the three highest letters and locate what they mean in the explanation grid at the end. The highest letters will be the gifts that you feel God has given to you. Work at these and become the best you can be.

Do not make this a tortuous exercise. Relax with it, do it with a friend and have a laugh. Then be released to be yourself!

1. I am handy at most things.
2. I get really excited at times in prayer meetings.
3. I enjoy speaking in front of a group of people.
4. I am deeply concerned about what is happening in the world.
5. I feel more comfortable in a youth meeting than in any other.
6. I feel real concern for people who are ill.
7. I find it easy to listen.
8. I often lead others to Jesus.
9. I sing a lot and really enjoy music.
10. I enjoy explaining things to others from the Bible.
11. People look to me for a lead.
12. I like administrative work.
13. I like helping other people.
14. I find that God just gives me a burden for a particular person at various times.
15. I love studying to prepare a message.
16. I am active in serving the community.
17. With the problems of today's society, I feel a special burden for the youth.
18. People seem to enjoy me being with them.
19. I find it easy to make relationships with others.
20. I love to talk to people about Jesus.
21. Others have said that I seem to be able to lead them into the presence of God.
22. People seem to be helped when I teach them things.
23. In a group I am often elected chairman or leader.
24. I have a clear head and am good at organising things.

25. I am the practical type.
26. Sometimes I have to just stop what I'm doing and come before the Lord in prayer.
27. I feel that God wants me to preach.
28. I am very aware of the needs of society today and want to do something about it.
29. Young people seem to be able to trust me and come with their problems.
30. I spend time praying with sick people.
31. I can encourage others and help them with their problems.
32. I find my life is full of opportunities to tell people about Jesus.
33. God has given me a clear musical ability.
34. I love study and finding out the facts.
35. I am good at delegating work to others.
36. I love office work.

| | | | | | | | |
|---|---|---|---|---|---|---|---|
| 1 | 13 | 25 | **A** | 7 | 19 | 31 | **G** |
| 2 | 14 | 26 | **B** | 8 | 20 | 32 | **H** |
| 3 | 15 | 27 | **C** | 9 | 21 | 33 | **I** |
| 4 | 16 | 28 | **D** | 10 | 22 | 34 | **J** |
| 5 | 17 | 29 | **E** | 11 | 23 | 35 | **K** |
| 6 | 18 | 30 | **F** | 12 | 24 | 36 | **L** |

My top letters are ________________________________

# Explanation Grid

| | | | |
|---|---|---|---|
| **A** | Practical | **G** | Pastoral |
| **B** | Intercession | **H** | Evangelism |
| **C** | Preaching | **I** | Worship Leading |
| **D** | Social Involvement | **J** | Teaching |
| **E** | Youth Work | **K** | Leadership |
| **F** | Healing | **L** | Administration |

# International Gospel Outreach

*'Recognising the whole church*
*& reaching out to the whole world'*

Kingsley Armstrong is a Trustee and President of International Gospel Outreach, which is a Worldwide Fellowship of Ministers, Christian Workers (of all kinds) and Intercessors, and gives recognition to God's calling on people's lives.

IGO was founded in June 1967 by a group of men, moving in the anointing of the Holy Spirit, with a burning desire to reach their generation with the Gospel of the Lord Jesus Christ. IGO still has 5 of its original 7 leaders, although several other key people have joined them over the years.

IGO is non-denominational in its approach, so all with the call of God on their lives and who are seeking to fulfil that call, are welcome, whether part of a 'recognised' denomination or not. It is totally committed to world-wide mission, to getting alongside key workers in the developing countries to support them in their calling and vision, and to being an encouragement to the body of Christ.

IGO strongly believes in the need for prayer & intercession and provides a 24-hour emergency prayer link, co-ordinated from its headquarters in North Wales. It seeks to encourage unity in the Body of Christ and promotes and supports Missions, Conferences & Conventions, Bible Seminars and Teaching at home and overseas as needed.

The IGO 'Nehemiah Bible Correspondence Course' provides vital training for those, particularly in the developing countries of the world, who cannot or do not have the means to attend full time Bible college. A diploma is issued on successful completion of the course.

Kingsley himself has developed powerful and exciting short courses called 'The Joshua Project' and 'JP2' and he holds these in the UK and on location around the world, releasing men and women of all ages into their God-given callings.

The Membership ARE IGO, and what they need, we try to provide.

IGO-linked Ministers and Christian Workers may or may not be Ministers within the denominational Churches. However, all Members must have a Church base to which they are accountable and committed.

The IGO base is located at the Oasis in Dwygyfylchi, North Wales and overlooks the seashore at the front and the mountains at the rear. All members and friends are welcome to visit and accommodation is available for short retreats, small conferences and individual breaks for those wanting to wait on God.

To find out more about IGO, visit **www.igo.org.uk**

For information about coming events or membership, send an email to **mail@igo.org.uk** or write to:
IGO
The Oasis
Ysguborwen Road
Dwygyfylchi
North Wales
LL34 6PS

Tel 01492 623629